Mama's Boy

Tom Garrott Benjamin, Jr.

Vision International Publishing, Inc.

Indianapolis • Palm Desert

Mama's Boy

All Scripture quotations, unless otherwise noted,
are taken from the King James Version.

Scripture quotations noted NIV are from the New International Version®, copyright 1973, 1978, 1984 by International Bible Society. Used by permission of Zondervan Publishing House.

Scripture quotations noted NKJV are from the New King James Version®, copyright 1982 by Thomas Nelson, Inc.

Scripture quotations noted NRSV are from the
New Revised Standard Version®, copyright 1989 by the Division of Christian Education of the National Council of the Churches of Christ in the USA. Used by permission. All rights reserved.

Scripture quotations noted TLB are from the
The Living Bible®, copyright 1971.
Used by permission of Tyndale House Publishers, Inc.,
Wheaton, Illinois. All rights reserved.

Any italicizing of Scripture verses is added by the author for emphasis.

Back to the Bible Publishing
P.O. Box 82808
Lincoln, NE 68501

Copy editors: Rachel Derowitsch, Kim Johnson

Cover and interior design: Robert Greuter & Associates

0-9712892-0-4

Printed in the USA

About the Author

T. Garrott Benjamin Jr. is a native of St. Louis, Missouri, and was raised in Cleveland, Ohio, by a single-parent grandmother. Since 1969, he has been senior pastor of the historic 3,000-member Light of the World Christian Church (Disciples of Christ), established in 1866 in Indianapolis, Indiana.

Dr. Benjamin is both an innovator and a motivator. His burden for young people birthed the first Respect Academy for children in the nation, and his burden for souls birthed the Tom Benjamin television ministry, and now, Vision International Publishing, Inc.

His ministry has been featured in the *Congressional Record, Washington Post, Jet Magazine, The Disciple Magazine,* and other national periodicals. Dr. Benjamin's ministry has also been seen and felt throughout the world through national cable television (TBN, BET, and LeSea) and the Armed Forces Television Network. He has preached on almost every continent, including speaking engagements and fact-finding tours in Australia, Cuba, and Russia.

Bishop Benjamin is also the founder of Project Impact Indianapolis, an intervention and counseling program for court-referred teens. He also oversees the New Directions Alternative Academy, under the auspices of the Marion County Juvenile Court, which provides discipline (boot-camp style) and academic education to teens who are referred by middle schools and high schools throughout Indianapolis. This short-term educational experience is the last stop for students who are on their way to expulsion and detention.

In February 2001, Light of the World Christian Church was named and recognized as one of the "best of the best" among 300 excellent Protestant congregations across the United States. The congregations were identified during the Parish/Congregation Study, a two-year research project funded by the Indianapolis-based Lilly Endowment. Researchers were based at the University of North Carolina at Wilmington.

Dr. Benjamin is host producer of the longest-running public affairs television program in Indianapolis, "Living for the City." He is a graduate of St. Louis University, in St. Louis, Missouri, and the Christian Theological Seminary in Indianapolis, where he earned his Master of Divinity and Doctor of Ministry degrees. He was inducted into the Board of Distinguished Preachers at Morehouse College in Atlanta, Georgia, and also holds several honorary degrees. His passion is children, and he has authored two other books: *Boys To Men* and *The Home Alone Syndrome.*

His pride is his family, consisting of his life partner, the beautiful and creative Lady Beverly, as well as three grown sons: Thomas III, Channing, and Christopher.

Table of Contents

Acknowledgments

First, I want to thank the Lord Jesus for saving my soul and making me whole. Then I want to thank my grandmother, Marilla Roberts Jackson, for picking up the broken pieces of my life and miraculously molding them into God's original design. She prepared my heart for Jesus to use my life. Her unselfish and unconditional love healed me and helped me to heal and help others. She even chose my wife, Beverly, who sweetens both my character and my coffee.

I would be remiss if I did not thank all who have touched my life and particularly my loving and supportive congregation, Light of the World Christian Church, for sharing and caring enough to allow me to write this book.

I want to thank Robert C. Larson, my editor and friend, whose gifts and graces are too numerous to mention. I am grateful to those who endorsed the early manuscript on blind faith, and to Alice Hord, my faithful secretary and friend, who typed every word and every chapter at least twice. God bless you all, and may your contribution help to "set the captive free."

Foreword

Here is a book that touches the heart. I have known Tom Benjamin for twenty-five years, and he has been both consistent and courageous on the subject of the rescue and empowerment of the family as a whole and children in particular. He is one of my dearest friends and, without a doubt, one of The Crystal Cathedral's favorite preachers. I believe he has shared his messages about the family and children at least ten times from the pulpit.

I could not put this book down. Even though our childhood differed, I could still relate to his love for his grandmother. I see the seed of "possibility thinking" being planted by Mrs. Jackson in my favorite chapter, "Love Is Not to Be Paid Back . . . but to Be Passed On," and I will eagerly tell you why. Ironically, it was in 1991 during the time "Mama's Boy" was preaching at The Cathedral that he received the heartbreaking news that his grandmother had gone to be with the Lord at the glorious age of ninety-four. He received the news a few hours before he was to preach, and he told me later that he was tempted to bow out, as he felt his tears may have made his preaching problematic. Instead, he preached like a man possessed on the subject, "Love is not to be paid back!" Wow!

This book will be recommended and read long after Tom and I have passed on from the scene. Its message glorifies God, empowers children who feel rejected, and confirms the fact that some of the best among us came from broken homes. It is a tribute especially to single parents who have lost hope and children of single parents who often feel rejected. Tom Benjamin has taken us on a faith journey that sets the captive free. Here is the *Man of La Mancha* with the impossible dream. Here is someone who dreamed the impossible dream and fought the unbeatable foe and won. Tom Benjamin turned his "hurts into hopes and his scars into stars." Mrs. Jackson must be proud of her boy today because he has made a difference in my life and so many others in his lifetime. Here is the story of self-esteem lost, regained, and then, most important, passed on. That is what I hope you do with this book— pass it on. It just may save somebody's life.

Dr. Robert H. Schuller
The Crystal Cathedral
Garden Grove, California

Prologue

I cannot express in words how much I needed to write this book. I was raised by a single-parent grandmother who actually gave her life for me that I might live for others. In an era of fatherlessness and single-parent prominence, I wanted to share my journey with the hope that it might help some single parent who has no help and is about to lose hope. I wrote this book for the millions of grandmothers whom God anointed to fill the gap left by disunity, divorce, or death.

I want to encourage every single parent and let you know that your labor in the Lord is not in vain. It is possible to raise a child successfully by yourself if you are wise enough not to try to do it by yourself. God has put so many helpers, seen and unseen, in our way as resources. The key is to identify them and use them.

I wrote this book to honor my grandmother, who gave all she had to insure my safe passage "out of Egypt." So many of us owe a great debt to our grandmothers, mamas, mam-maws, nanas, and big mamas. I just hope that this Mama's Boy has done something to let my mama know that I am grateful.

I wrote this book for the millions of boys and men, past, present, and future, who are fatherless but not helpless or hopeless. I want my brothers to know how blessed they are to have a mother or grandmother to care for them and to cover them. I want them to know how we should never take for granted the gifts of God. It is important for all of us to realize that no one has to do anything for us, and when they do we should be grateful.

This is the story of a rejected boy who became a respected man of God by the grace of God and a *grand* grandmother who gave her all. This is Tom Benjamin's journey, and you will find yourself in it too.

It is a love story that touches the heart. It can be summed up by Mama's mantra: "Love is not to be paid back, but to be passed on."

Tom Benjamin
Indianapolis, Indiana
2001

Introduction

T. Garrott Benjamin Jr.—the name rings with a definite and decided euphony. I heard the name before I met the man, and the euphony escalated as our friendship and mutual respect continually grew. My first impression, upon meeting Tom, was his unbounded enthusiasm for his work and his witness. I immediately discerned the source, for authentic enthusiasm stems from *en theos* (in God). And that's the key to *Mama's Boy*.

This book is one of those rare productions that had to be. Such a pilgrimage, replete with parental rejection, youthful innocence bordering on helplessness, Grandma's reception, and her inculcation of love, hope, and Christian values—all of these working together to shape and mold a young man into one of God's stars in a dark world—herein lies the miracle of grace.

With absolute candor, courage, and commitment, Tom tells the story of his odyssey, and always in the picture, whether in substance or in shadow, is that lady of rare grace and gentility—Grandma Marilla Jackson. She typifies that figure so prominent in the lives of some and so urgently needed in the lives of many others—THE OTHER MOTHER.

Read this book again and again. Let the words walk in Kipling manner: "up and down the avenues of your heart." They speak with the eloquence and the urgency that produce pleasure out of pain. They reflect the essence of the legend of the Thornbird, namely, "the best is bought only at the price of great pain."

William Augustus Jones
Bethany Baptist Church
Brooklyn, New York

Chapter One

ST. LOUIS BLUES

*When my father and my mother forsake me,
then the LORD will take me up.*
Psalm 27:10 (KJV)

*Life is best understood backwards,
but it must be lived forward.*
Søren Kierkegaard

I can still see the steam rising from the underbelly of the enormous black locomotive as my parents escorted me to a platform at the St. Louis, Missouri, train station, where a waiting engine was hissing and convulsing as it made itself ready to take the overnight journey to Cleveland, Ohio. Where were my parents taking me? Why had we not discussed this trip to wherever? Why was I dressed in my Sunday best—little suit, cap, and oxford shoes so highly polished I could almost see my face in them? I didn't recall my folks saying we were going on a vacation. Perhaps this was meant to be a surprise—a family outing, a few well-deserved days away from the office for my father, a leading dentist in the African-American community, or maybe a break for my mother, who spent her days bemoaning the fact that she was now trapped at home with a baby. She never had to work outside the home, but seemed unable to make the adjustment to being a mother.

As we walked closer to the train, my heart beat faster as my worst nightmare suddenly became reality: *Tommy, you're going to your grandmother's house. She'll be waiting for you at the station. And she'll take real good care of you. So don't you worry, Son, it's going to be all right. You're going to Mama's (our name for Grandma) house, (which was not so bad as long as you did not have a one-way ticket).*

Confused and mystified

Mama's house. Mama's house? For how long? My heart
leaped at the idea that I'd be gone for only a few days or
weeks, but my young mind told me it might be for a lot longer
than that. Little by little, the Holy Spirit seemed to be whispering to me that I would be boarding that train never to return.
Down deep I knew something was up and that I had in my
pocket a one-way ticket to Cleveland. Confused and mystified, I
threw my arms around my father and mother and said what I
wondered might be a final good-bye. I remember no tears. A
red cap helped me into the train, since my legs were too short
to negotiate the steep steps. I remember how he gently picked
me up and escorted me to a sleeping car. I recall the silence of
the moment as he showed me to my temporary home—an
upper berth on a train bound for Cleveland. Nothing was said,
and I said nothing, for I was only five years old.

**Little by little, the Holy Spirit seemed
to be whispering to me that I would be
boarding that train never to return.**

If this were a film, it would now call for an exterior shot,
with the camera slowly zooming in on a bewildered little
black boy, whose face and hands were pressed hard against a
cold train window as he strained to catch a final view of his
parents on the platform below. The closeness of the shot
would reveal sadness, confusion, pain, and rejection as the little boy was frozen in time—his well-scrubbed face glued to
the window. Perhaps if he pressed hard enough, the glass
would give way and he would again find himself in the arms
of his parents, thus ending his nightmare. But it was not to be.
The shrill sound of the conductor's *All Aboooooard* interrupted his brief reverie—along with any realistic hopes for a
reunion with his mother and father.

The train began to groan down the tracks, slowly picking

up power as it left the station, the steam of its locomotive making its presence known and obscuring the little boy's view of anything or anyone on the platform. Ever hopeful, he pressed his face and hands still harder against the pane as the only world he knew faded into a steam-shrouded distance. He hoped to capture a final view of his mother and father. But they had either left the platform or the vapor from the locomotive had blanketed them from sight. The little boy sensed his parents were already walking to their automobile, not waiting any longer than necessary to get on with their lives. They were now free. For whatever reason, Tommy Benjamin was suddenly aboard a train for Cleveland and on his way to an adventure at Mama's house. He was, confused, puzzled, alone. And he was only five years old.

Rejection and abandonment

There are many facets to pain; it is such a complicated reality. Sometimes pain is sharp and sudden; at other times it's dull and numbing, and you can seldom predict it. It comes from disorder and "dis-ease." As I boarded that train for Cleveland, I remember thinking, *This is not something I asked for.* It is something I don't fully understand even today. I do know, however, if you leave people—children especially—uncovered, unprotected, uncared for, and exposed to uncertainty and fear, you leave them vulnerable to being hurt for a lifetime. Rejection usually precedes the process of being uncovered, and whether we abandon babies at birth, through abortion, or after birth, there will always be pain. In the end, someone will pay an enormous price.

Although I cannot recall many details, I suspect that the first five years of my life were agonizing because my parents were in pain and their relationship was dysfunctional. I know there was an inordinate amount of fighting and emotional turmoil while my mother was carrying me. This mayhem continued long after I was born. It's an awful thing to be able to remember the confusion and chaos of the first five years of your life. I remember two instances that were especially traumatic. One was a tremendous fight that raged between my mother and father. I don't remember how old I was when it occurred, but I know the hostility and abuse of that event was intense and disruptive to a little boy not yet five years old. The angry interchange in the bedroom that day between my parents was so harsh and hostile that I remember putting my hands over both ears and going down into the basement to get as far away from the confusion as possible.

**I was so sick. I just wanted to be
touched, loved, cared for.**

Another event was equally upsetting. I remember lying in my crib one night with some kind of illness. I don't know if it was a childhood disease, such as chicken pox or whooping cough, but whatever was afflicting me was pushing my temperature sky high. The house we lived in was large, and I was lying in a small crib in a very large room. I was so sick. I just wanted to be touched, loved, cared for. What I got, however, was a mother and father who left me alone to go to a party. As I lay there, I remember my parents engaging in yet another heated exchange, with words such as, "Oh, come on, he'll live. He's not gonna die. It'll be okay if we leave him for a while." At that moment, I remember the room got bigger, the crib smaller, the room darker, and I became increasingly afraid because I was all alone. I felt no one who really cared much about me.

My next childhood memory was being put on the train to Cleveland.

Busy parents

My father was raised in Montgomery, Alabama. He worked his way through college, and then again labored to pay his way through the Meharry Medical College in Nashville,

Tennessee—ironically as a dining car waiter on the railroad. He began the practice of dentistry in St. Louis sometime in the early 1930s. Through a mutual friend he met my mother, who was living at the time with my grandmother in Cleveland. He was at least twenty years older than my mother. When you think about the period in which my father lived and worked, it becomes obvious that here was a black man who had to be someone special to attain the status of one of the youngest professionals in the city with his own practice. He had impeccable taste. He was highly respected as a man of character, integrity, and uprightness within the community. With him, there was not a shred of looseness or moral impropriety. My parents married in 1941. I was born in 1942.

My father was a great success in his field, and he reaped early material rewards for his labors. He always drove a new Cadillac and always lived in a nice large home, although I never knew him to be extravagant with either his affluence or influence. The only home I remember living in with my folks was a white brick house on Vinegrove Avenue off of Taylor Avenue in inner-city St. Louis. The house had plenty of yard and a patio porch extending from the side.

While most of my childhood memories reside on the side of the traumatic, there is one experience that still brings a smile to my face: my parents bought me a pet goat. Other kids had dogs, cats, hamsters, and birds. Not me. No, *Tommy had a goat*, and it was my goat's calling in life to pull me around the yard in our cart. One night the goat broke loose from his pen and found his way over into a nearby basement, where he tore up all the neighbor's clothes and had them for a late- night snack. It was a neighborhood scream: "Tommy's goat ate up Sis. Jennings' clothes." It was a big thing. I don't remember being blamed for the goat's forcible entry into our neighbor's cellar, but I do remember the confusion that followed in trying to find the goat. I also remember it was the end of the goat. But not even my short-lived yet happy acquaintance with my friend the goat could counterbalance the lack of love and affection from my parents.

One day I heard my folks say, "Look here, we just don't need an extra burden around this place, and that's what Tommy is... a burden—both to us and to our career. I want to live my life. The only sensible solution is to just give him up and send him off to live with his grandmother. That should do it!" Even if I'd never heard such a conversation, I would have detected their disaffection with me through their actions. *Sticks and stones may break my bones, but it's your lack of love that hurts me.* I think I now understand what the Danish theologian Søren Kierkegaard meant when he said, "Life is best understood backwards, but it must be lived forward." For example, as I look back on my father's life, I feel I've gained a greater respect for who he was and what he was trying to do—in the only way he knew how to do it. That's why I'm able to forgive him for what I felt he did to me. I still believe he abandoned and rejected me. But now I better understand how difficult it would have been for him to raise a son alone. He was not a nurturer. He was not a warm, sensitive person. He was a driven, upright, successful professional who would not make anyone ashamed of him in any way. He simply had no sense of what it meant to be a father. The world is full of men like him, and I have tried not to be like that but I am never sure I succeeded.

I prayed for years just to hear the words
***I love you* come from my father's mouth.**
Unfortunately, I had to wait until he
lay on his deathbed before he uttered them.
It was really good to hear them, but they
were decades too late. And then
maybe it's never too late.

Forgiveness is one thing; residual pain is another, and I do not think that childhood heartbreak will ever be eradicated from my life. I prayed for years just to hear the words *I love you* come from my father's mouth. Unfortunately, I had to wait until he lay on his deathbed before he uttered them. It was really good to hear them, but they were decades too late. And then maybe it's never too late. That's why *I love you* are three words that I speak easily, freely, and many times a day—to my wife, my sons, the members of my congregation, my cherished colleagues, and now to you, my reader friend. *I do love you ... and there is not a thing you can do about it! You might be on the way, but you are never in the way. You are precious and you are a prize—a one-of-a-kind miracle and an unrepeatable historical event. And don't you forget it.*

Looking back, I believe my father's releasing me to my grandmother may have been more of an act of grace than anything else. I now know "that in all things God works for the good of those who love him, who have been called according to his purpose" (Romans 8:28, NIV).

And then there was my mother, Faith Jackson Benjamin. Now this may sound like a riddle, but I'm grateful that I was raised by my grandmother and not by my "mother's mother." Confusing at first, perhaps, but here's what I mean. I'm glad my mother's mother was not my mother, but that my mother's mother, who was my grandmother, *became* my mother because she changed as a woman as she grew older and came to love me even more toward the end than at the beginning. My birth mother, Faith Jackson Benjamin, would never have been able to do that. My grandmother loved me, chose me, accepted me, *and wanted me when my real mother wanted nothing to do with me.* But her problems did not originate with me. My birth mother's life was shaped by a spirit of rebellion. And painful as it was to see happen, I feel I actually benefited from watching my mother self-destruct. My mother didn't seem to know that she had any choices.

She went to public schools and graduated from Howard University. She was a brilliant person: well read, well liked, but forever an insurgent. She began drinking early in her teenage years and started smoking even earlier—up to two packs of Camels a day for her entire life, along with her habit of drinking death-defying amounts of liquor. She would put "Old Grandad on a Camel" every day. Unhappily, she carried those addictions into a marriage that already had more than its share of challenges. She was a woman in pain and in trouble. But it still takes "two to tango," because an insensitive, compulsive man is no better. People cannot be selfish and defiant and be happily married, because a lifelong commitment requires that wives submit to their own husbands, and that husbands love their wives (even when their wives have not matured to the submissive stage) as Christ loved the church and gave Himself for it (Ephesians 5:24–25). Both husbands and wives must be constantly giving and forever forgiving. They must yearn to obey God and yield to each other. But woe to the marriage if rebellion rules in the heart of either. A lazy man or a controlling woman is not just an enigma, but also an anathema—the antithesis of what God designed for a healthy, life-giving marriage. Marriage is about submission to God and the Word of God, and then to one another. Marriage is a divine institution that is ordered and blessed by obedience and submission to God first, and then the rest becomes doable.

**Marriage is all about *give* and *forgive*.
How I wish my parents had known that secret.**

When a person brings his or her adolescent scars into a marriage—something easy to do if not warned—that individual will pay the price by perverting and polluting the relationship. Selfishness and rebellion are twin demons that haunt all men and women, and must be avoided at all costs. They are to be confronted early and conquered quickly. It was a terrible problem in my family; it may be a problem in yours. Marriage is all about *give* and *forgive*. How I wish my parents had known that secret. As the old song says, "You have to give a little, take a little, and let your poor heart break a little. That's the story of, that's the glory of love."

Private tears

As the train picked up speed, I finally turned away from the window, where the scenery was now changing every few seconds. My brain was trying to keep up with the swift-moving events of the last few minutes; so were my emotions. Feeling as if I had no control over what was happening, I sat down in the seat, stunned, and in childlike confusion quietly wondered what was happening to me. In my mind's eye I could still see my parents in their finery saying good-bye on the train station platform. As I slowly settled into my unfamiliar quarters, I remember feeling so very alone.

The next memory I have is getting prepared to go to bed and hearing a porter say something like, "Don't worry, you won't fall out of bed, because there is a safety net to keep you from falling. That's right, there's a safety net right here. You'll be just fine." A safety net? If I fell, I would be rescued. Little did I realize how prophetic those words *safety net* would soon become. I'm sure someone had told the porter to watch after the little boy in the upper birth *because he's going to his grandmother's house, and he needs someone to take care of him.* Little did I know that I was entering into an awesome adventure that was going to change my life completely.

Except for that kindly, ebony-skin gentleman in the black uniform with gold buttons getting me ready for bed, I had little, if any, exposure to anyone else on the train. I just remember boarding the train, getting ready for bed, falling asleep, and arriving in Cleveland early the next morning. In some ways, going to visit my grandmother was an awesome adventure—not a traumatic experience, even though I was beginning to put two and two together based on some of the things I'd heard my parents talk about. Perhaps it was because of the hostility and antagonism I'd known for so long in my home that I felt as if I were being released from prison, or perhaps a tomb. I sensed I was escaping something bad and was on the verge of departing to a better place, where I would be loved unconditionally, where there would be no fighting and yelling. Did I cry? Yes, I cried. But they were silent tears, private tears—a breathless sort of cry.

Years later, the thought registered that even as I crawled from that upper berth the morning we arrived in Cleveland, I was at the same time experiencing another kind of birth—a new birth, and a new life. I did not know what the future held for me, or who would take care of me or for how long. I just knew I was going to Mama's house in Cleveland for a visit—a place where I would be safe and loved.

William Christopher Handy, the world-famous "Father of the Blues," was born November 16, 1873, in a small log cabin on the west side of Florence, Alabama. During the early decades of the twentieth century, Handy helped nurture a musical sound that proved to be both mournful and moving—a sound this young black musician would simply call "the blues." The composer once described the expressive texture of his music as "the sound of a sinner on revival day." Handy's most famous composition, "St. Louis Blues," was published in 1914, twenty-eight years before I was born. While he could not have written his song with me in mind, over the years "St. Louis Blues" also became my song—mournful, soulful, and a reminder of the trouble I'd seen in this sleepy but famous town on the banks of the Mississippi. As the clickety-clack of the train's mighty wheels put me to sleep that night, I was leaving St. Louis behind. But the "blues" of loss, confusion, and bewilderment would remain part of a little boy's heart and soul.

At that point, however, how could I possibly know what really was happening to me? I was only five years old.

Chapter Two

GRATEFUL TO BE A MAMA'S BOY

*Train a child in the way he should go,
and when he is old he will not turn from it.*
Proverbs 22:6 (NIV)

*Loving can cost a great deal;
but not loving always costs infinitely more.*
T. G. Benjamin

I f you can think of an upper berth in that sleeper car as a womb connected to a train bound for Cleveland, then you can imagine the darkened cavity from which I was about to emerge.

I still remember the rhythmic clickety-clack of the train wheels that put me to sleep—a sleep with no dreams, no nightmares, and no memories. A little boy bound for Cleveland slept soundly throughout the night. If you've ever traveled by train for any distance, you know how hypnotic the sounds of the great steel wheels and the gentle rocking of the train car as it snakes its way to its destination can softly and sweetly hasten slumber.

Starting over at five years of age

During that brief journey from St. Louis to Cleveland, God gave a confused little boy peaceful, restful sleep in preparation for his new life in this new place. I've always been grateful to a loving God for His provision and protection that night. It was a gift from above. But all good things must come to an end, and early the next morning my new life in Cleveland would begin—whether I was ready for it or not. In God's special way, I think He used the stillness of the night to prepare me to get off that train and climb into the waiting heart of someone who loved me. The shrill sounds of my parents' incessant quarreling had begun to take its toll: I would not miss the anger and the conflict. I had been told too often, both in angry words and in dispassionate actions, that "Tommy was always in the way, and that Tommy was interfering with the more important professional interests of his parents, and that Tommy was either not wanted or had been a mistake." I was glad to receive a reprieve from the uncertainty and chaos of my first five years of life.

> **The shrill sounds of my parents' incessant quarreling had begun to take its toll: I would not miss the anger and the conflict. I was glad to receive a reprieve from the uncertainty and chaos of my first five years of life.**

As the train approached Cleveland, and as the porter, my new best friend, helped me descend the ladder from an upper berth that seemed two stories high, I realized I was crawling out from my temporary living quarters healthy, happy, and very much alive. I remember how I literally I jumped out of that dark "womb" in anticipation of starting a new life. I don't know what happened to me during my sleep that night on the train, but when I awoke, I recall that my mind was filled with such thoughts as, *I wonder if I'll ever go back home.... I think I may have seen my mommy and daddy for the last time.... I hope I'll like it in Cleveland.* There may have been other thoughts, but I don't remember. I was only five years old.

Now, finally dressed and ready for the train to pull into the station, I remember how I began craning my neck to look out of the window where nothing was familiar. *What would it be like when I got off the train? Who would take care of me? Would my grandmother be there to welcome me to a new place?* The screeching of the wheels desperately grabbing at the rails interrupted my reverie as the locomotive hissed towering stacks of steam, and as the couplings between the passenger cars were forced to test their linkage once again, proving they could stay connected. With one final lurch the train stopped. Whistles blew, and the sounds of many voices stabbed the air. My heart beat wildly as I strained my eyes to look for love that I prayed would be in the shape of a grandmother. I pressed my nose to the window for the last time, moving my eyes from right to left, left to right, up and down. *Would she be here? Would she really be here to meet me? Would I be disappointed again? Would I be rejected again?* I couldn't take another rejection.

Filled with the excitement of knowing I would soon be among the passengers leaving the train, I picked up my little travel bag and prepared to leave the sleeping car. That's when I heard the porter say, "Look, Tommy, is that her? Tommy, that is your grandmother right there. Come on, let's go. She's waiting for you!"

With my tear-filled eyes glued on my grandmother, I ignored the last step and leaped into her waiting arms, only to hear her tearfully, but cheerfully, say, "How's Mama's boy?"

The porter didn't realize I'd already seen my grandmother pacing back and forth as the train pulled into the station. She was close, but still so far away. My heart was pumping fast, and my eyes must have been larger than saucers. I remember I couldn't get off that train fast enough. The porter took me by the hand and escorted me out of the car to the top of what appeared to be a mountain of steps beneath me. He made sure that I was the first one off our car. I looked down on the platform, and there she was, waiting for me—my little sweet grandmother, only five feet tall, wearing a tattered coat, and with a face that radiated the welcome message, *I really love this little boy.* When I arrived at the top of the small staircase, the porter held my hand as I took one step down, and then another. With my tear-filled eyes fastened on my grandmother, I ignored the last step and leaped into her waiting arms, only to hear her tearfully, but cheerfully, say, *"How's Mama's boy?"*

"How's Mama's Boy?"

I remember thinking, *I made it. I'm home, Mama, I'm home.* It would be the beginning of a new life for Tommy Benjamin, a little boy who, in only a few hours, had gone from rejection to redemption, from being lost to being loved, from being abandoned to being adored. Yet I had no idea what the future held for me. How could I? I was only five years old.

A woman ahead of her times

My grandmother, Marilla Roberts Jackson, was an unusual person. In a society sinfully segregated by race, she was a graduate of Howard University, a writer, editor, publisher, landowner, a businesswoman, and entrepreneur extraordinaire. She owned a large double home at 10532 Bryant Avenue in the Glenville section of Cleveland's eastside with her husband, who died about the time I was born. She lived in one half of the property and rented the remaining half, which was a common practice at that time. Her boarders were single men, most of whom worked for the Cleveland Transit System, the railroad system, or the local post office. The house was built with two separate entrances.

Grandma Jackson's business acumen was legendary in Cleveland. She started her life of commerce by renting four or five single rooms upstairs in her home. From that small beginning, she used her carefully saved money to purchase several other houses throughout the city, which she owned and managed as rental property. I remember she once had as many as five large homes in Cleveland that were rented at all times. As I grew older, I remember often making the rounds with her to collect the rent from her growing number of tenants. It was my first introduction to the world of business—Marilla Jackson-style.

> **My grandmother had long since broken
> the mold of the stereotypical black female.
> She, like Madam C. J. Walker, the first black
> female millionaire, represented a unique
> breed of the women of color.**

Black women at the time were neither expected nor encouraged to be skilled in the world of business. However, my grandmother had long since broken the mold of the stereotypical black female. She, like Madam C. J. Walker, the first black female millionaire, represented a unique breed of the women of color. How could anyone dispute that she was unique? Her business prowess spoke for itself. With her capable hands already involved in enough enterprises to produce burnout in most executives, she still found time to purchase and manage a building that held both the offices and the printing press for the *Cleveland Herald*, of which she was the publisher. This newspaper was at one time the second-largest African-American weekly in Cleveland. Her editor, Mr. Ormond Forte, was a graduate of Oxford University in England and had come to Cleveland from England via the West Indies. The two of them ran the paper successfully for about ten years, during which time my grandmother wrote a weekly column and later published her own book, *Life's Crossroads*—an amazing book that consisted of many *little things* about which she had more than a casual opinion. So you will be better able to catch a glimpse of the wisdom, love, and spiritual discernment of the little woman who welcomed me that morning in Cleveland, I want to share with you what she once wrote about "Imagination and Gratitude."

Sunday, while taking a drive, I passed a palatial home, beautifully landscaped—its grounds adorned with exquisitely made garden furniture. It was exceedingly picturesque.

I remarked to my friends who were riding with me that the place was a scene of "heaven on earth." To look at that estate, one would think that all of life's wishes for happiness should be bundled up right there.

But, are they?

Maybe the occupants of that home are so busy worrying over what other luxuries of life they do not possess that they fail to get the true joy of what they have. Maybe there is lacking in that home what is ordinarily so easy to obtain if we will, and that is a peaceful mind and grateful heart.

When I speak of a peaceful mind and grateful heart, I am thinking of people who could be happy, but they allow their imaginations to run away with them in the direction, which brings confusion rather than peace.

Marcus Aurelius once wrote: "Our lives are dyed the color of our imaginations." A student of psychology will also quickly tell you that our imagination is stronger than our will. We so often rob ourselves of the true joys and happiness of life by directing our imagination the wrong way.

Imagination plays an important part in our lives every day. From morning until night, it's imagination or expectation that keeps us going. When we capture our imaginations, we certainly accomplish much. Whether it be good or bad that is entirely up to us, for imagination is stronger than the will.

But if the mind is filled with wholesome thoughts and interesting suggestions, those appetites and habits, which they are trying to escape, will be crowded out.

Then there is the question of the grateful heart to think about.

We are so busy reaching out for more of everything that we forget to be thankful for anything except when reminded. If those people who live in that beautiful home, about which I last wrote, are grateful, of course their home is then a "little heaven on earth." And the same goes for our own lives.

Yes, if we thanked Providence more and appreciated our blessings more, the happier we would be. And if we learn to stretch our imagination towards something that will benefit us, we will find ourselves living in a "little heaven of our own." For as I often say: Life can be beautiful—if we would let it be.

Happiness comes from within, and gratitude and imagination are great stimulants toward it.

Footsteps in my heart

That was my grandmother, Marilla Jackson: articulate, excellent, strong, entrepreneurial, God-fearing—and now she was Mama. I used to pronounce it "Mam-Maw" up until I became a teenager, when I changed to "Mama." Whatever I called her, she always answered—and that was a blessing. Little did I realize I was walking through an amazing doorway that would lead to an unspeakable richness of life: to the joy of being loved; to the thrill of being chosen; to the importance of being disciplined; to a freedom from fear; and to a peace of mind that would pass all understanding. Best of all, *I was Mama's boy.* Only years later would I appreciate the words of Phyllis A. Wallace, the first African-American female to receive a doctorate in economics from Yale, who said, "The kind of ancestors we have is not as important as the kind of descendants our ancestors have." I can tell you that my grandmother would have made all our ancestors proud indeed—not only because of her enormous talents and boundless energy, but also because she chose to put much of her life on hold to take in a little boy who'd been turned aside by his parents because he'd somehow gotten in the way of their success plan.

My grandmother knew what it was like to value children; she understood that we all suffer immeasurably if we do not recover, restore, and redeem the boys and girls in our lives—as well as those on the periphery of our lives.

My grandmother knew what it was like to value children; she understood that we all suffer immeasurably if we do not recover, restore, and redeem the boys and girls in our lives—as well as those on the periphery of our lives. She knew children are not only our future, but also our present. She taught me: "Adults are history and children are destiny." When you save a black boy, you save a black man. She knew that adults needed to help children "start out the way they wanted them to end up." She knew that because children were valuable to Jesus, they should also be valuable to her. She understood that it is the duty of all adults not to pick *on* children, but to pick them *up* and pick them *out* so they can bless those who've been abandoned, abused, or neglected. Instinctively, she knew that grandmothers are angels who lift us children to our feet when our wings are too weak to fly. Over the years, many wonderful people have walked in and out of my life, but my grandmother left footsteps deep in my heart. How else could a rejected little boy ever have grown up to become a respected man of God? It was all the making of my Heavenly Father and my saintly grandmother: those two, together, made all the difference in the world.

Many years later when we paid off the mortgage on my first church, Second Christian Church in Indianapolis, I was twenty-six years old and had followed a beloved twenty-six-year pastor named R. H. Peoples. I led the great people of that church to pay off the mortgage within nine months, and we remodeled the church for more than a quarter of a million dollars. My grandmother gave a $15,000 electric sign that was put on the corner of 29th and Illinois. I had the signboard read: "Thank God and Grandma."

Children are for loving

As you read these words, you read them either as a mama, a daddy, a mama's baby, daddy's baby, a mama's boy, or a mama's girl. Perhaps you were never separated from your birth parents. I hope you've not had to endure the heartbreak of boarding your own train and climbing into your own upper berth on your way to your own unknown land. But if my story is also your story, then you and I really do understand each other, and together we will seek God's healing in these pages by embracing our pain and allowing it to redeem our present.

As I write these words, I've just heard the news that a teenager in Santee, California, a suburb of San Diego, has just been taken into custody after shooting up his high school campus. When the boy was finally arrested—with eight bullets remaining in his .22 pistol—thirteen lay wounded; two of the best and brightest in that school lay dead. That young man was also a mama's boy—a deeply troubled mama's boy. Apparently, along the path of his young, tortured life, someone stopped loving him, stopped affirming him, stopped telling him he was special, stopped showing him—through loving action—that he was a unique creation of a loving God. I don't know the reasons for today's tragedy, but my heart goes out to every boy who is fatherless and every child who feels hopeless—especially to those mama's boys and mama's girls.

**If my story is also your story,
then you and I really do understand each other,
and together we will seek God's healing in these
pages by embracing our pain and allowing
it to redeem our present.**

Here's my fear: I'm terrified of a society that continues to treat children as *disposable*—used and unvalued, to be cast aside to make way for something *more useful.* We see it in the wholesale marketing of children by greedy and unconcerned parents, a media motivated by greed, the propagation of pornography, a miserable misuse of hip-hop, rap, rock, and other forms of music that shout hate, rape, misogyny and homophobia, prejudice and fear. Where is it all headed? What is the fate of our children who must endure this exploitation and abuse? And what about those thousands of children who do not have the privilege of living with a Marilla Jackson, or a loving parent who dares to discipline and lives to love?

My grandmother was a successful businesswoman—but she refused to put property before people. She was compassionate, not calloused. She refused to chase the American dream at the expense of a five-year-old boy who needed a mama. She was always there for me, and if she wasn't around, I can assure you the neighbors suddenly emerged as my surrogate parents. *They treated me as if I were their own child.* That meant if I needed a spanking, they exercised that privilege, with the full approval of Mrs. Jackson. Yes, it does help to use the whole village to raise a child—but it must be the right kind of community, where the quality of the moral and spiritual leadership is beyond reproach, and people do their utmost to care for children, especially during their formative years.

She refused to chase the American dream at the expense of a five-year-old boy who needed a mama.

Whether it is a William J. Clinton, a George W. Bush, a Jesse Louis Jackson, a Jimmy Carter, a Richard Nixon, a Colin Powell, or an Arnold Schwartzkopf—all these men were adolescents and every one was once a little boy, a *mama's boy.* No one becomes a man or a woman without first becoming a boy or a girl. Every adult is preceded by an adolescent. As a result, how we impact and influence *our children* has everything to do with the quality of our national life and our public leaders. It is still true: "as the twig is bent so grows the tree."

And so we weep over America. It's time to weep. We have willingly neglected America's greatest resource: our children. Some of our children are truly lost, waist deep in their own desires, and cut loose from their moorings. Too many of our children feel there is no hope. Still, they are all mama's boys and mama's girls, and what they need most is love, acceptance, affection, and *someone to meet them at their own train stations of life with that "how's Mama's boy" look in their eye.*

Compassion makes all the difference

Yesterday I received a note from a friend that contained one of the most intense stories I've read in many days. It hit me especially hard, I suppose, because as I read it, all I could think was, *This young man was also a mama's boy.* Here's the story.

One day, when I was a freshman in high school, I saw a kid from my class walking home from school. His name was Kenneth. It looked like he was carrying all of his books. I thought to myself, Why would anyone bring home all his books on a Friday? He must really be a nerd. I had quite a weekend planned, so I shrugged my shoulders and went on. As I was walking, I saw a bunch of kids running toward him. They ran at him, knocking all his books out of his arms and tripping him so he landed in the dirt. His glasses went flying, and I saw them land in the grass about ten feet from him. He looked up and I saw this terrible sadness in his eyes. My heart went out to the guy. So, I jogged over to him as he crawled on the ground looking for his glasses. I saw a tear in his eye. As I handed him his glasses, I said, "Those guys are pitiful. They really should get a life!" He looked at me and said, "Hey, thanks!" There was a big smile on his face. It was one of those smiles that showed real gratitude.

I helped him pick up his books and asked him where he lived. As it turned out, he lived near me, so I asked him why I had never seen him before. He said he had gone to private school before now. We talked all the way home, and I carried his books. He turned out to be a pretty cool kid. I asked him if he wanted to play football on Saturday with my friends and me. He said yes. We hung out all weekend, and the more I got to know Kenneth, the more I liked him, and my friends thought the same of him. Monday morning came, and there was Kenneth, with his huge stack of books again.

I stopped him and said, "Boy, you are gonna really build some serious muscles with this pile of books every day!" He just laughed and handed me half the books. Over the next four years, Kenneth and I became best friends. When we were seniors, we began to think about college. Kenneth decided on Georgetown, and I was going to Duke. I knew we would always be friends and that the miles would never be a problem. He was going to be a doctor, and I was going for business on a football scholarship. Kenneth was valedictorian of our class. I teased him all the time about being a nerd. He had to prepare a speech for graduation. I was so glad it wasn't me having to get up there and speak.

On graduation day, I saw Kenneth. He looked great. He was one of those guys who really found himself during high school. He filled out and actually looked good in glasses. He had more dates than I had and all the girls loved him. Boy, sometimes I was jealous. Today was one of those days. I could see that he was nervous about his speech.

So, I gave him a "high five" and said, "Hey, big guy, you'll be great!" He looked at me with one of those looks, and smiled. "Thanks," he said. As he started his speech, he cleared his throat, and began, "Graduation is a time to thank those who helped you make it through those tough years. Your parents, your teachers, your siblings, maybe a coach, but mostly your friends. I am here to tell all of you that being a friend to someone is the best gift you can give them. I am going to tell you a story."

I just looked at my friend with disbelief as he told the story of the first day we met. He had planned to kill himself over the weekend. He talked of how he had cleaned out his locker so his mom wouldn't have to do it later and was carrying all his stuff home. He looked hard at me and gave me a little smile.

"Thankfully, I was saved," he said. "My friend saved me from doing the unspeakable."

I heard the gasp go through the crowd as this handsome, popular boy told us all about his weakest moment. I saw his mom and dad looking at me, and smiling that same grateful smile. Not until that moment did I realize its depth.

So this reminder: never underestimate the power of your actions. With one small gesture you can change a person's life. For better or for worse. God puts us all in each other's lives to impact one another in some way.

It's true . . . for better or for worse, one small gesture can change a person's life—a child's life. For me, the seemingly small gesture of a little grandmother who made the effort to pick me up at the railway station in Cleveland, Ohio, altered my life's direction. Now, half a century later, at times I will still lie in bed and wonder about that train ride. What if my grandmother hadn't shown up? What if those arms had not been there for me? What if I had not heard those life-changing words: "How's Mama's boy?" I really miss my Mama.

Chapter Three

IT TAKES A WHOLE VILLAGE

*Verily I say unto you, Whosoever shall not
receive the kingdom of God as a little child,
he shall not enter into it.
And he took them up in his arms,
put his hands upon them, and blessed them.*
Mark 10:15-16 (KJV)

It takes a whole village to raise a child.
African Proverb

Mrs. Marilla Jackson was brilliant, disciplined, hard-working, well read, and could "read you" well. And because of her enormous life experience, she had no problem understanding what Charles Dickens meant when, on the eve of the French Revolution, he wrote, "It was the best of times. It was the worst of times." She understood it because she knew it's *always been like that*. She chose to believe the times were always good; she'd also long ago figured out the times would always abound with roadblocks. She saw the paradox and was aware of the tension. She lived with—and even embraced—the dissonance, and while I was in her care, she taught me to understand the same. She taught me that we enjoy unprecedented growth in the superficial, while we find ourselves deficient in what should be the substantial. She helped me understand that we had "taller buildings, but shorter tempers; wider freeways but narrower points of view." She saw people buying more and enjoying it less. She could see the brilliant minds of our nation conquering outer space, while being defeated on the battleground of our inner being.

So what, she figured, if highly educated astronauts could walk on the moon and still be able to communicate with NASA, and yet regular folk couldn't go down the street and be able to talk to another human being who happened to be black, brown, red, yellow, or white? My grandmother saw people cry *freedom*, and yet remain uptight. She was around when brilliant scientists split the atom, but she saw little progress with people severing prejudice and removing racism.

Grandma saw people with more degrees and less common sense, and she was astute enough to notice that we were long on quantity but short on quality. She saw big churches and little Christians; big meetings and little ministry; big religion and little Gospel.

She saw people with more degrees and less common sense, and she was astute enough to notice that we were long on quantity but short on quality. She saw big churches and little Christians; big meetings and little ministry; big religion and little Gospel. Over the years her thoughts have become my thoughts—how could they *not* be? I lived with my grandmother, sat with her, went to church with her, prayed with her, was disciplined by her, and learned everything worth learning about life from her—and I praise God for her influence on my life. That's why not a day goes by but what I'm grateful that I was Mama's boy.

Marilla Jackson did not overtly demonstrate much affection to me or to anyone else. I don't have many memories of her hugging or embracing me very much, particularly as I got older. That wasn't her style. However, she gave me an even greater gift than physical touching or constant approval: her undying affection came through in her willingness to do anything for her chosen child, Tommy Benjamin Jr. *Anything!* After all, I was Mama's boy—and I still am. From the day she picked me up at the train station until the day she died, she poured her life into mine.

Prudent and passionate

It did not take long for her heart to become my heart; her soul, my soul; her thought patterns, my thought patterns; her concerns, my concerns. She was a prudent provider and passionate protector for a little boy who was working through the rejection he still felt from his parents. My grandmother knew what I needed, when I needed it, how much I needed, and she was always there to give it to me. Those times when I displayed an antisocial attitude or a sullen spirit, she would say with a firmness that told me I was in big trouble, "Tommy, come over here a minute. We need to pray." And my how we did pray . . . until the glory of God came upon us.

Day after day she prayed with me, she prayed on me, and she prayed over me. And when she would stop praying, one of two things would always happen: either she would let me go, or she would say, "Tommy, this ain't workin'," and she'd pick up something—usually a switch from a tree in the back of our house—and apply it to an area of my anatomy where I would most remember it. She was the president of the *"Board* of Education."

My grandmother had an exceptionally short fuse, and there was never much time to recover after words such as, "Tommy, did you hear what I said?" or, "Don't look at me with that tone of voice," came out of her mouth. Marilla Jackson moved fast, and she never suffered fools gladly. I either did what she asked me to do—on *her* timetable—or I would pay the price—big time, every time. Still, I never felt she was abusive or cruel. Sometimes hardly tolerable, yes, but upon reflection, I'd have to admit I probably deserved everything I got. She could have coined the term *tough love*, because that was what she was all about one hundred percent of the time. She could be real tough and real tight, but I always knew she loved me, and she never labored discipline. In other words, she got it over with. *Praise God, she got it over with!*

She used the whole "village"

Now you've got to understand something that's very important. My grandmother was an excellent entrepreneur. She was a hotel founder and owner. The Hotel Thomas in Cleveland was located on the "gold coast" of the city's nightlife at 105th Street and Massey. It was named after me—after all, I was Mama's boy. While she owned a newspaper and was a successful entrepreneur, *she still had me to contend with*. So how did she handle her mounting responsibilities and business decisions, and still feel confident that I, the child into whom she was pouring her life, was being properly raised?

I was an only child, but I was never alone.

Very simple. She understood better than anyone I've ever known that it took an entire village—a village called Bryant Avenue between Superior and St. Clair in the Glenville area of Cleveland—to raise a child. That's what she believed, and that's what she relied on. If my grandmother wasn't around, she knew others would be, because they had all been "deputized" to serve as my mothers and fathers, just as every child on that street, known for its family environment, was designated as my brother or sister. I was an only child, but I was never *alone*; I had once been a castaway, but on Bryant Street I became one of the family. The "village" and the "villagers" looked after me day and night, and it gave a little boy the security and sense of refuge he needed right from the start—when he was only five years old.

Because of the outpouring of caring and discipline that came from that little village, I felt loved, accepted, cherished, and adored. Because my Mama got her strength from her walk with the Lord Jesus Christ, I know she was continually blessed by the words of Scripture—especially by those powerful portions of God's Word where Jesus spoke, without hesitation, of His feelings about children. Among others, Mark records the scene in chapter 10, verses 13–16:

> And they brought young children to him, that he should touch them: and his disciples rebuked those that brought them. But when Jesus saw it, he was much displeased, and said unto them, Permit the little children to come unto me, and forbid them not; for of such is the kingdom of God. Verily I say unto you, Whosoever shall not receive the kingdom of God as a little child, he shall not enter into it. And he took them up in his arms, put his hands upon them, and blessed them.

A heart tender toward children

That's what my grandmother did to me: she blessed me, and blessed me, and then blessed me some more. That's all she knew how to do. And because I have been so blessed, my life-long prayer continues to be that I, in my ministry, will pass that blessing on to others.

In 1975, I wrote a song while I was working on my doctorate at the Christian Theological Seminary in Indianapolis, Indiana, called "Blessed to Be a Blessing." The chorus goes like this:

> I've been blessed to be a blessing
>
> I've been saved to do some saving
>
> I've been loved to do some loving
>
> And I want the world to know
>
> What a blessing it is to be blessed.

That's why my heart is so tender toward the children in our society who are being battered instead of blessed and who live in fancier houses but broken homes—where they are as disposable as diapers, and where there is much in the "show window, but nothing in the stockroom." My grandmother was determined that such would not be my fate, and because she sensitized my heart with her unconditional, uncompromising love, my ministry has always been to share my passion and my position to help rescue and empower our children.

More than ever, I'm convinced *this is the key to our future* and the *solution for our confusion*. Someone has said that life is like a can of sardines, and everyone is looking for the key. Now, as an adult—and still proud to be Mama's boy, and eager to perpetuate my grandmother's life of love for the little ones in our midst—I would propose that the key to our better future is in the Master's mandate to make children a priority instead of a program. That's what the spirit of the Gospel according to Mark 10:13-16 is all about.

In this passage, we experience the Master's heart on one of the most important issues He ever addressed—the manner in which we treat children in our society, and in the church, an issue that is inextricably bound to the issue of racial reconciliation and the racial future of our nation. When it comes to the future, the richest resource our nation has is the next generation, our youth. If we neglect the next generation, we abuse our future. That's why, if you want to predict the future of our families, our society, and our nation, simply observe what we do to and through our children. Look at what we teach them, tell them, and sell them. The racism, violence, and greed—that tyrannical triad of pain—has a chokehold on our nation and our cities, and it will never be broken until we are willing to *get the mind of Christ* concerning our children. We might as well admit, as I have often said, that *adults are history, and children are destiny*. Our boys and girls are not so much lost as left; not so much ornery as abandoned; not so much niggardly as neglected; and not so much out of control as overwhelmed by a flood of foolishness and fakery that is thrown at them by the media and maniacal men who manipulate their minds with the mess of this age instead of the message of deliverance.

> **Our boys and girls are not so
> much lost as left; not so much ornery as
> abandoned; not so much niggardly as neglected;
> and not so much out of control as overwhelmed
> by a flood of foolishness and fakery that is thrown
> at them by the media and maniacal men who
> manipulate their minds with the mess of this age
> instead of the message of deliverance.**

Raise a child; save a nation

My grandmother listened to the radio; she knew what was going on, and, for the most part, she didn't like what she heard: *That's why she needed a village to help raise me*. She knew that she, a single black woman, would never be able to carry out the enormous task of raising a child alone. My grandmother read the daily newspaper, poured over the editorials, devoured the columns—and wrote many of them herself. She didn't always like what she read: *That's why she needed a village to help raise me*. Today, if I tell you things are worse now than they were then, I wouldn't be telling you anything you didn't already know. Of course things are worse today than they were in a little "village" called Bryant Avenue in 1947. A lot worse. Many American cities have become the murder capitals of the world, with children killing children, the abused growing up to carry out even more abuse, and runaway gangs ruining the lives of innocent children.

And there's a reason: *teenagers are out of control because we as adults have failed to exercise control*. We call them delinquent, but rather it's we who are derelict. It's time to quit blaming the victim and get to the source of our pathology. The Bible has it right when it pleads the case for us to train a child . . . raise a child . . . save a nation. I thank God that my grandmother understood this, because without her disciplined love and caring, there's no telling how a little boy from St. Louis might have ended up.

You may say, "Well, this may all be true, but, in all honesty, the problem you describe just doesn't affect me. I'm listening to you, but at the same time, I need to respectfully disagree. What was once a family problem has become a neighborhood problem, which has become a city problem, which has become a state problem, which has now become a national problem." I have come alongside you in this book to say that if we are to solve our problems—and they are all our problems—we must hear and *do* the Gospel just as my grandmother did, by investing more in our young people, by making them a priority from the day they are born—even while they are in the womb. The days of simply finger-pointing to malicious music, raunchy rap, sordid sex, and all other manner of the devil's devices that divide, destroy, demonize, and damn our children are over. The buck stops on *your* shoulders and mine—adults, fathers, mothers, uncles, aunts, brothers, and sisters.

For that reason, we are wise to embrace the African proverb, "It takes a whole village to raise a child." The government can give a child a free lunch, but it takes the church and a caring adult to give him Jesus. A head start without a changed heart is an exercise in futility. People's morals and values—or lack of them—and spirituality and compassion—or lack of it—were carefully shaped during their adolescence, not in adulthood. Liars, bigots, racists, totalitarians, drug lords, murderers, prostitutes, and cheaters are not *born.* They are *made,* and again "*as* the bough is bent, so grows the tree." I began to learn this at the knee of my grandmother—when I was only five years old. I'm now considerably older, and the message has not changed. But the message has changed me, even as it can change you.

Not only a village . . . a *healthy* village

Marilla Jackson knew we needed the home, our schools, the government, and the church all to work together—all the time: when it was easy, and when it was difficult; when there was cooperation, and when there was confusion. She knew one person or institution could never handle the challenge alone. She knew *it took a whole village to raise a child.* She knew Dr. King and Martin Buber were right when they agreed that what *affects one directly, affects all indirectly. I can never be what I ought to be until you are what you ought to be.* And if my grandmother were writing this, I know she would say something like, "Before we throw heaps of blame on the 'obvious offenders,' let's look first into our own hearts for what is amiss, to our own homes where we have devalued a child, and into our own churches, where, for the most part, we have segregated children out of our Sunday worship and made them second-class citizens, set apart from the life of the church and community."

"Let's look first into our own hearts for what is amiss, to our own homes where we have devalued a child, and into our own churches, where, for the most part, we have segregated children out of our Sunday worship and made them second-class citizens, set apart from the life of the church and community."

Mrs. Marilla Jackson knew *it takes a whole village … a healthy, helping, happy, holistic village … to raise a child.* Back then time was not on her side. Today, we have even less time to love our children, and the hour is fast approaching midnight. As a matter of fact, it's 11:55 p.m.

However, if we fail to heed the tender words of our Savior, we put ourselves on the precipice of losing it all. Hear again the Word of the Lord: *And they brought young children to him, that he should touch them: and his disciples rebuked those that brought them.* Let's assess our position and confess our negligence. What are we doing individually and as churches to bring our children to Jesus—which is a far greater and more important mission than simply bringing them to Sunday school? Because to bring children to Jesus is to bring them to the Truth.

Jesus and children

But when Jesus saw it, he was much displeased, and said unto them, Suffer the little children to come unto me, and forbid them not: for of such is the kingdom of God. I can still hear my grandmother's voice as she would read this passage aloud, and then, without words, to see her act out the message of her Savior by passionately reaching out to children—starting with me, a little boy she had chosen to bring into her home and her life to be loved and nurtured.

Verily I say unto you, Whosoever shall not receive the kingdom of God as a little child, he shall not enter therein. I hope we can agree that our position in regard to children will always be based on the condition of our minds and our attitudes. The writer of Proverbs presses home the point: *As [a man] thinketh in his heart, so is he* (23:7). That's the key—to find, feed, and nurture the mind of Christ—and Christ's mind is on the side of a child, whose attributes are equal to the mind of His Kingdom: humility, honesty, happiness, and hope.

And he took them up in his arms, put his hands upon them, and blessed them. You and I, if we are to be those loving, compassionate "villagers" who help raise our children, support our children, and discipline our children in the ways of the Lord, must be willing to pick up our boys and girls and bless them—not just professionally, but personally, in the name of Jesus, to help lift the heavy loads that have been forced on their young shoulders, and to help raise those up who have fallen because *we have let them down.* But before we can pick one up, *we must pick one out.* Surely, charity begins at home, but today I challenge you who are childless or even empty nesters to pick out and pick up a child of another color or culture and open up your hearts and homes to make a friend. I also encourage you to use the money God has given you to support and invest in organizations that are "picking up" children: your church, Project Impact, Boys and Girls Clubs, Pal Clubs, inner-city summer camps, and Big Brothers and Big Sisters.

Keeping life in perspective

One hundred years from now, it will not matter how much money you and I had in the bank, how well we did in our roller-coaster relationship with the Dow Jones average, where we lived, how well we lived, or what kind of cars we may have driven. What *will* matter is the eternal difference we made in the life of a child—something you and I can never do alone. *We were neither designed nor mandated to go solo on such an important mission.* It will take all of us—all the time—because *it takes a whole village to raise a child.* Jesus understood this—perhaps because of the pain of rejection He experienced in His own childhood. I know that's why I understand it. My compassion for children is a passion prompted by my own heartache and inspired by my single-parent grandmother, who took Jesus seriously. My passion for children is fueled by my pain. I, along with Smokey Robinson, say, "Follow the tracks of your own tears. Whatever makes you cry, you have been assigned to heal." When my mother and father divorced when I was five, and my grandmother stepped in to be that first "villager," she made a lifelong commitment to me. And it didn't matter that she was barely five feet tall and wore a tattered coat when she arrived at the station to pick me up . . . nor that I was only five years old.

That's because caring for another person—child or adult—has nothing to do with physical appearance, the quality of clothing, or any amount of things the world deems of value. Instead, caring has everything to do with blessing someone whose heart and soul are opened wide, and who extend an invitation to leap into the arms of Jesus. *When your mother and father forsake you, the Lord will take you up*... something that usually happens when someone takes Jesus seriously, and who understands that it takes a whole village to raise a child.

Raise a child, restore the family, save a city, and bring hope and redemption to a nation. Our children are our seed, and every seed has the potential of a forest. But will it be a chaotic jungle of wild weeds or a woodland of sturdy oaks? Will it be weak plants blown away with the first wind of fall, or a strong, supple humanity with God-given strength to endure the challenges life has to offer?

Whenever Satan wants to thwart the divine purpose of our Heavenly Father, he directs his attacks on the seed of the next generation—our children.

Throughout the Bible, whenever God wanted to fulfill His divine purpose, He would arrange for the birth of a child—a Moses, Jacob, John the Baptist, Mary, Martha, or Jesus. Conversely, whenever Satan wants to thwart the divine purpose of our Heavenly Father, he directs his attacks on the seed of the next generation—our children—whether through an Oklahoma Federal Building or a Columbine High School. If we refuse to learn from the errors of our past and present, those who follow us will be condemned to repeat those transgressions. However, when we, as the larger *village* of loving, compassionate, caring adults, plan for the future of our children, and when we as *villagers* work actively toward making our communities a better, nobler, more blessed place for our children to live, truly the kingdoms of this world will become the kingdoms of our Lord and God, and He shall reign forever and ever.

Chapter Four

START OUT THE WAY YOU WANT TO END UP

If your child asks for bread,
do you trick him with sawdust?
If he asks for fish, do you scare him
with a live snake on his plate?...
you wouldn't think of such a thing.
Matthew 7:11 (The Message)

Never mention the word "failure." Always accentuate the positive.
Earl Woods, the father of Tiger

Today, throughout our society, there are many mama's boys and girls who stand in pulpits, sit in palaces, live in presidential houses, maintain positions in industry, and occupy places of great distinction; there are also many mama's boys and girls who are wasting away in our nation's prisons and penal institutions. Why is this? Why are so many redeeming the time, while thousands of others are *doing time?* Why are so many of these men and women national treasures, while others are national throwaways?

To answer my own question, I submit that it is essentially because of the vision their parents had of their children's future—or lack of it. All parents, you and I included, live and model a lifestyle that is more caught than taught. It's an old saying, but still true: *What you do speaks so loudly that I can't hear what you are saying.* Therefore, is it any profound psychological mystery to understand that a child who is forced to sit in his daddy's van until midnight while his father is drinking in the local bars just might become an alcoholic? By the same token, is it so difficult to believe that parents who monitor their children's activities, help them with their homework, pray over them night and day, trust them into the arms of Jesus, *and*

51

help them start out the way they want them to end up will not have a different kind of child, adolescent, and adult?

Caught more than taught

I thank God for so many things I learned from the generous heart and righteous spirit of my sainted grandmother. But as I review my life with her, I realize I, too, probably *caught* more than I was *taught.* While she had her pet phrases and her standard ways of disciplining me, she didn't give me a lecture every day on how to live my life. She didn't have to. I *caught* her principles in action. I *caught* the way she gave to others who had little or nothing. I *caught* the way she welcomed people into our home—where she talked to them, listened to them, fed them, and always did what she could to help make their lives better. Without my realizing it at the time, she was helping me start out like she wanted me to end up. What a powerful principle. It is not just being Mama's boy that determined what I became; it was the interaction I enjoyed between a single-parent grandmother who showed me the way.

Was it easy for her? I don't think so. She had a happy, productive, successful life long before I arrived on the scene. But once she said to my parents, "Send Tommy to me," she found time in her busy schedule to be the person God wanted in my life— and she did it with love, discipline, prayer, *and a daily dose of good values that I could see invading every part of her life.*

How my grandmother lived in my presence could well be a model for every parent in America and around the world. She didn't wait until I was grown up to "suggest" that I develop good values. I saw them from day one. And when I'd get off track and need an attitude adjustment, she would look me in the eye and say, "Tommy, now you listen to Mama. I know you don't want to do what I tell you sometimes, but *you've got to start out the way you want to end up."* And I can still hear those words echo in my mind today . . . *start out . . . start out . . . the way you want to end up . . . the way you want to end up.*

When I was young I couldn't understand the importance of what she was telling me. Later I did, as I do today.

Model the kind of future you want to see come to pass for your child.

So my challenge to you, my friend, is this: put my grandmother's philosophy in place in your home, with your children. It's not too late. Model the kind of future you want to see come to pass for your child; *be* more than *do*. Let the Person of Jesus Christ so capture your heart that you will think of your child's future from the rising of the sun until the sky becomes dark. Pray for your child and ask a merciful Heavenly Father to protect, preserve, and safeguard your child. Pray *with* your children so they will have the experience of you calling on the Lord on their behalf. It will be a lesson they will never forget. Praying *for* them is not enough. We must pray *with* them. Please don't say it's impossible. It may be difficult, challenging, painful—but never impossible.

That idea will never work!

I remember once reading several historical examples of how the experts of the day regarded certain new ideas and inventions as impossible, unworkable, dangerous, and outright foolish—all things we now consider commonplace. Here are four such examples:

1. In Germany, "experts" proved that if trains went as fast as fifteen miles an hour—considered a speed no human could possibly withstand—blood would spurt from the travelers' noses and passengers would suffocate when going into long, dark tunnels. In the United States, experts said the introduction of the railroad would demand the building of hundreds of insane asylums since people would be "driven mad" with terror at the sight of locomotives.

2. When the idea of iron ships was proposed, experts agreed they simply would not float, would damage more easily than wooden ships, that it would be impossible to preserve the iron bottom from rust, and that iron would play havoc with the readings of the compass.

3. The New York YMCA announced typing lessons for women in 1881, only to be confronted with vigorous protests that "the female constitution would break down under such enormous strain." (By the way, my grandmother won a national Smith-Corona typing contest in the 1930s.)

4. New Jersey farmers resisted the first cast-iron plow, invented in 1797, claiming the cast iron would poison the land and stimulate the growth of weeds.

We laugh at these "impossible" situations because we know the criticism was ill advised. But what was in the minds of the inventors? Long before Stephen Covey coined the phrase "They saw the end at the beginning," they would not be dissuaded from their vision and their passion. So when you think that raising a child is impossible, think of the future of that child and how you want him or her to end up.

But you say, "Dr. Benjamin, you don't know my situation. I'm a single mother. I work. I'm burning the candle at both ends and am trying to figure out a way to light it in the middle. I don't have time to think about my child's future. I'm just trying to survive the present." I hear you and sympathize with you. Perhaps you need the help of a "village"—your church, your group of friends, your parents or relatives—to help raise your child. You don't have to go it alone. However, whatever behavior you model and encourage your child to model now is how, in all probability, your child will end up. I know you want that to be a future of hope and joy. Whatever you do, don't give up! Hang in there—Jesus did!

Breaking the cycle of pain

If we do not think of our children's better future, we will

never break our children's cycle of pain—that ache in our hearts that we have produced and caused them to live with.

**It is pain that pain produced;
a hatred that hatred has produced;
a violence born of violence. It is not fair to
blame our children for their devious ways—
when, for the most part, they are ending up
just as they were started out.**

It is pain that pain produced; a hatred that hatred has produced; a violence born of violence. It is not fair to blame our children for their devious ways—when, for the most part, *they are ending up just as they were started out.* In my case, I had the potential to miss the train. For me, it could have gone either way. I still wonder what would have happened to a little five-year-old if my mama's mama had not picked up the torch and said, "What you won't do for my child, I must do for you"—and, because of her decision to choose me, my grandmother became my mother. That's why my story may well be *your* story because, in all likelihood, someone one day came into your world—a grandmother, an "auntie," a relative, a coach, a teacher, a pastor—and said, "This child won't make it unless I step in. I must help him. He will need to start out the way he wants to end up."

I doubt if my grandmother ever used the now-familiar word *boundaries,* but she knew a great deal about them: she set them in place for me, had high expectations that I would honor them, and had a foolproof accountability plan firmly in place to deal with me if I chose to ignore them. And she had her plan ready to go, in advance. Why? *Because she wanted me to start out the way she wanted me to end up.* She knew what was acceptable, and what was not—and so did I. As Dr. James Dobson wisely says, "If you haven't defined it, don't enforce it!" Early on, my grandmother was already *focusing on the family—a healthy, accountable, responsible family!*

And I am not alone. I think of the many millions of children of every hue in the rainbow, and particularly those of color, who can affirm the power of the presence of a godly grandmother or aunt who picked up the torch of raising them in the ways of the Lord. For thousands—me included—with no help but the help of the Lord, the options would usually be either a prison or a pit. Everybody needs somebody to help them steer clear of the pit and, when we find ourselves in the pit, to help us get out it. What so often seems like "man intends for evil, God intends for good."

I'm thinking now about the story of Joseph, where his own family threw the young man into a pit to die. As a matter of fact, his brothers even considered killing him, jealous as they were of Joseph's abilities, skills, charisma—and being favored by their father. Let us slay the dreamer and see what shall become of his dream, they mocked. From the plotting of their act of treachery to the moment they threw Joseph into the pit, their intentions were evil, but God had another plan. Never forget Joseph's justice lesson: "You meant it for evil, but God meant it for good." We know the rest of the story of how Joseph became a leader in all of Egypt, a man of great influence.

**Never forget Joseph's justice lesson:
"You meant it for evil, but God meant it for good."**

But note this. It took someone else to raise him. Someone else had to step in to nurture him, train him, educate him, and take care of him when his parents were far away. And it is no different for us or for our children today who need to be rescued from the pit of sin, ignorance, prejudice, anger, despair, and fatherlessness. If we do not protect our children, provide them ways of escape, and present options of care and concern—whether they be from our own parenting or from someone in our family or society who steps in to help—we run the risk of killing the dream and the dreamer, because where there is no hope, there can be no dreams.

Prayer changes you and me

But what can I do to make a difference? Perhaps your greatest contribution to the welfare of our children is to pray for America. Pray for your family. Pray for a nephew or a niece or a grandson or a son. Maybe that's all you can do, but I don't believe you if you say you can do nothing, because prayer changes things; and if you pray long enough and strong enough, prayer will eventually change you.

Perhaps you are raising a child you have never truly valued. Maybe it's a child you have already raised, but because of your drive for material benefits, you put your most important possession on the back burner to be successful with others, rationalizing that *it was my way of making sure my child had everything he or she needed.* But in the process of gaining money and things, you didn't expose your child to positive people and programs, you did not patiently wait for them when their little feet moved too slowly, or pick them up when they fell to the ground, or talk to them when they had a minute to spare. You did not hold them when it was all they needed, or hug them when it would have meant the world to them, or sacrifice for them because it would have interrupted your schedule. I know of what I speak, because my parents saw little Tommy Benjamin as one who stood in the way of their career. I have long since forgiven them, and emotional scar tissue has grown over much of my pain, but there's still enough residual sadness left for me to try to help others not to make the same mistake. Parents, love your children unconditionally.

If you feel the guilt of past actions, the good news is that there's still time to do something to help raise up a child who needs your love. Maybe there's a boy or girl in your family or in your community who has no one to pick them out and pick them up. Perhaps they are in a foster home or are up for adoption. Perhaps it's a child who's been bullied, put down, and told he or she is worthless. Whoever they are, wherever they are, you still have time to help a child start out right so he or she will end up right, something for which the time is always right. I simply urge you to do what God is asking you to do to help lift up a child so that he or she will begin to see through windows of hope rather than from the dark edge of the pit of despair.

Love in action

It is not my purpose to pass judgment on anyone who reads this book. But I would be remiss if I did not speak the truth in these pages in a spirit of Christian love. That's why I can ask the questions, do you—did you—as a male or a husband, insist your wife work when you could have really lived off one income? Because of your drive for material things, did you promote the home-alone syndrome? Are your children still waiting to have a few precious moments with you? America and its parents will have to repent first of wanting things before they want family; of wanting things before they want character in their children and morals in their adolescents. No mistake about it: we will pay the price for not praying with *our* children. As I said before, we say we pray *for* our children, while, honestly, some of us can only remember the last time we prayed with them was when they were in a crib where we prayed the childhood prayer, "Now I lay me down to sleep ..." By the way, that prayer still works, particularly if you carry it all the way through adolescence.

Are your children still waiting to have a few precious moments with you?

Just as it takes a whole village to raise a child, *it takes a parent's whole heart to give a child all he or she needs.* Too many of our little ones live their entire lives without their parents sitting on the couch or in a chair to talk and listen to them. Too many of our children have only heard "grace" at meals, but have felt no grace at any other time. Some have never heard their parents pray, and pray, and pray until tears flowed down their cheeks, and until they felt God's presence in the room. Why is it—and I'm as guilty as the next person—that we feel it unnecessary to pray with them? Oh, we pray for them briefly in our own personal and private devotions, *but we never pray with them … over them … around them … above them … and beneath them.* God forgive us for not praying with our children.

You can't begin a morning nutritionally deficient and expect a healthy, positive result in the evening. We have raised a spiritually deficient and malnourished generation. As a result, we are paying a great price.

If child rearing is anything, it is intensely practical, for there is nothing theoretical about changing dirty diapers or coping with a child's tantrums. For example, if you send your child out without a nourishing breakfast, that's a false start. You can't begin a morning nutritionally deficient and expect a healthy, positive result in the evening. A mother who cares about a little one wakes the child up gently and feeds that child with as much positive affirmation as she feeds him a nutritional breakfast. A loving father tells his little girl that she's a child of God, that this is the Lord's day, and that everything she touches this day has been created by Him—*and for her.* Together, loving, giving parents send their child to school with the words echoing in the little one's ears, *You are somebody. You are God's child. Enjoy your day, and come back this afternoon with some results of a great day.* Parents will do this *if* they recognize the importance of helping their children start out the way they want them to end up. When we give our children no start, it is unrealistic to expect them to cross any finish line with dignity or self-respect. If they do not respect themselves, how will they respect others?

I taught my sons as well as the children of African descent in our church the Respect Creed, which I wrote. It goes like this:

The Respect Creed

Praise the Lord! I am somebody!

I am God's child; I am somebody!

I am black, I am beautiful, I am bold, I am blessed . . .

AND I AM FREE!

We do not have to agree, but I must respect you

And you must respect me!

I respect my history, I respect my country,

I respect the law and the flag,

I respect my teachers and authority.

I respect every religion, race and creed . . .

I hear what you say, but I respect your deeds.

We do not have to agree, but I must respect you,

And you must respect me.

I respect mother Afrika, I respect Step-Mother America.

I respect Nelson Mandela. I respect Bishop Tutu.

I respect Martin, Malcolm, Medgar, and Elijah Muhammad;

I respect my pastor, and I respect my church.

I respect Frederick Douglas, Harriet Tubman, Nat Turner,

Sojourner Truth, Denmark Vesey, Crispus Attucks,

Langston Hughes, James Weldon Johnson, Marcus Garvey,

W. E. B. DuBois, And Carter G., Booker T., Madame

C. J. Walker, and all the rest ...

I RESPECT EXCELLENCE ... I EXPECT THE BEST!

We do not have to agree, but I must respect you,

And you must respect me!

I am God's child.

I am black, I am beautiful, I am bold, I am blessed,

AND I AM FREE!

We do not have to agree, but I must respect you,

And you must respect me!

You are not the target

My grandmother used to tell me, "Tommy, you have to be careful how you leave the house each morning, because your attitude in leaving the house will affect every person you come in contact with for the whole day." I didn't understand her reasoning at the time. I do now. She used the example about the paperboy who'd go down the street delivering papers. The basket on his bicycle was filled with his papers, and he'd just throw as hard as he could in front of each house on his route. Well, one day he threw a paper and it broke the window of the storm door. It was 4:30 in the morning, and the man of the house woke up to crashing glass. His wife, fearing it might be a burglar, demanded that her husband bravely get up to see what happened. He had gotten in late the night before and he didn't feel like going downstairs, but he finally did. He went to discover the paperboy had thrown the paper through the window—obviously by mistake. The paperboy was going on a Boy Scout trip, and he was delivering the paper two hours early that morning. So there the man was, surrounded by broken glass, angry, and later unable to go back to sleep. "From that point forward," my grandmother said, "the man's wife caught the blues, his dog caught the blues, his secretary caught the blues, the waitress at lunch caught the blues, and the gas station attendant caught the blues—and not one of them was the target.

The real target was the little boy who threw the paper, who was off to camp not knowing the ripple effect of his action."

I heard that story over and over, her reminder to me that you can get upset about something and attack everyone else all day about something that is not their problem. It's *your* problem, she would remind me. "So, Tommy, get your problem all straightened out before you leave the house, and then have a good day." Then, dead serious, she'd say, "Tommy, you know you can have a good day if you want to. So make up your mind to have a good day. Hup, wait, what's that look on your face? Hold it. Let's take another picture of that. Come on back. Let me see some joy. Come on. Tommy, do we need to pray?"

And so it is with life. You are not always the target, but you and I are affected by both attitudes and actions that have a ripple or echo effect, whether we are the paper boy or the awakened man. Watch your attitude and your actions when it comes to your children. They will imitate both.

This soldier ended up right

Integrity was my grandmother's middle name. She said what she meant and, I can assure you, she meant what she said. When the chips were down, everyone could take her at her word. She neither equivocated nor shaded the truth. And that's the legacy she poured into the heart of little Tommy, who suddenly appeared at her doorstep.

As I was thinking about the importance of integrity in our lives, my mind went back to a story I read about a young soldier who exemplified that quality in an unusual way. My grandmother never heard this story, but if she had, she would probably have said, "Tommy, that's it. That's what it means to be a person of your word." It's the true story about Lt. John Blanchard, a young soldier in basic training in Florida during World War II.

One evening he wandered into the Army library and found a book to read. As he worked his way through the book he became quite impressed, not with the content of the book so much as with the notes penciled in the margins. The feminine handwriting showed insight and understanding as well as a touch of tenderness. He flipped to the front of the book and found the name of the previous owner, a Miss Hollis Maynell.

Blanchard did some research and found out her address was up in New York. He wrote a letter to her, and the next day he was shipped overseas. For thirteen months the two of them corresponded by letter, and during that time they began to open their hearts to each other. It soon became apparent that they were falling in love. One time he asked her to send him a picture, but she refused, saying if he really loved her it really would not matter what she looked like.

Finally the day came when they were to meet. They arranged to meet each other at Grand Central Station in New York at 7:00 on that particular night. She told him, "You'll recognize me by the red rose that I'll be wearing on my lapel."

At a minute to seven the soldier straightened his uniform as people walked toward him, his heart pumping with anxiety and anticipation for this long-awaited meeting. From here on, let me describe what happened in his own words.

"A young woman was coming toward me, her figure was long and slim, her blonde hair lay back in curls from her delicate ears, her eyes were blue as flowers, her lips and chin had a gentle firmness, in her pale green suit she was like springtime come alive. I started toward her entirely forgetting to notice that she was not wearing a rose. And, as I moved in her direction, a small provocative smile curved her lips: 'Going my way, soldier?' she murmured. Almost uncontrollably, I made another step closer to her, and then I saw Hollis Maynell.

"She was standing almost directly behind the girl. A woman well past forty, she had graying hair tucked under a worn hat. She was more than plump; her thick ankled feet were thrust into low-heeled shoes. But, she wore a red rose on the rumpled brown lapel of her coat. The girl in the green suit was walking quickly away. I felt as though I was being split in two; so keen was my desire to follow her and yet so deep was my longing for the woman who's spirit had truly companioned me and upheld me during those months overseas. And, there she stood. Her pale, plump face was gentle and sensible; her gray eyes had a warm and kindly twinkle. I did not hesitate. My fingers gripped the small, worn, blue leather copy of the book, which was to identify me to her. This would not be love, but it would be something precious, something perhaps even better than love, a friendship for which I had been and must ever be grateful.

"I squared my shoulders and saluted and held out the book to the woman, even though while I spoke I felt choked by the bitterness of my disappointment. 'I'm Lt. John Blanchard, and you must be Miss Maynell. I am so glad you could meet me here; may I take you to dinner?' The woman's face broadened in a tolerant smile. 'I don't know what this is all about, son,' she answered, 'but the young lady in the green suit who just went by, she begged me to wear this rose on my coat. And, she said if you were to ask me out to dinner I should tell you that she is waiting for you in the big restaurant across the street. She said it was some kind of test!'"

Chapter Five

NO TEST, NO TESTIMONY

*We fall down, but we get up. A saint is just
a sinner who fell down but got up.*
Donnie McClurkin

*For though a righteous man falls
seven times, he rises again.*
Proverbs 24:16 (NIV)

Someone very wise once said the people who win have usually been counted out several times, it's just that *they didn't hear the bell.* These folks are invulnerable. They've been tested by fire, tried by turmoil, and put up against such insurmountable odds that no one thought they could possibly survive, much less thrive. They've been left at their own railroad platforms, wondering what's going to happen down the tracks. These people of courage know that the difference between success and failure is the ability to get up just one more time than you fall down. They understand you either invest your life in *something*, or you throw it away on *nothing*—and that the struggle is worth the price. They also know they dare not live on negativity, obsessing on what they're against, but that they must remain driven by what they are for, tough and challenging as such a philosophy may be.

My grandmother was one of those people who knew all about testing and being tried. She lived a life of absorbing the heat, and she never, for a moment, was afraid of leaving the kitchen. She also knew—and she taught me from those first weeks she took me under her strong but gentle wing—that if there were no test, there could be no testimony. She said the two went hand-in-hand: always did, always would. By her disciplined, creative, active, God-honoring life she demonstrated to me each day what Dr. Robert Schuller would say years later: *Don't kill your dream; execute it!* And what marvelous dreams she dreamed for me as I observed her Christlike actions day after day. I thank God my grandmother never saw herself as a victim, not even during those years when America found itself embroiled in intense racial turmoil—not to imply that the struggle is any less intense today. But anyone who was not asleep at the switch knows that the fifties and sixties were especially tumultuous years for African-Americans.

Grandma stayed positive

Marilla Jackson was fully aware of the testing that was coming down. She saw it, smelled it, felt it, and wrote about it. She knew that because of discrimination, per capita income of blacks was well below that of whites; that because of Jim Crow we were not as well educated; and that because of segregation we lived in rundown neighborhoods where crime was high. My grandmother knew as much about civil *wrongs* as she did about civil *rights*. Yet she was not a complainer about what might be going wrong; she always found a way to do it right, and make things right. *And don't you forget, Tommy, if you have no test, you'll have no testimony.* Little did I realize at the time how profoundly accurate my grandmother was. No test, no testimony, and I might add: "no mess, no message."

My grandmother knew as much about civil *wrongs* as she did about civil *rights*.

But it was not only the formidable challenges facing African-Americans that riveted her attention. She had a much more expansive view of historical events and of the enormous, weighty lessons to be learned from the Word of God. Among my fondest memories are when she would open her well-worn Bible and read me captivating stories of the great men and women throughout Scripture, especially those who struggled to be the persons God had created them to be. People such as Moses, who could have thrown in the towel at any time. After all, he was a boy whose childhood was "interrupted," after which he was taken to live in a foster family. Moses lived with a violent temper, had a tongue he could barely control, and posted a criminal record that should have put him away for good. *But Moses met the test, Tommy, and that's why he had the kind of testimony we are still reading about today. You, too, will be tested. You can count on it.*

When she finished talking to me about Moses, she'd often shift to a man called Peter, another solid soldier of the cross who struggled valiantly to make the unconventional transition from the profession of fisherman to fisher of men. Headstrong, outgoing, gregarious, and "me-first" by nature, one day he tried the ultimate trick: walking on water *under his own power.* As the water began to rise, he was reminded that he'd failed to keep his eyes on Jesus—something that, even today, will always provide a certain *sinking feeling.* Time and again, Peter could not seem to get it right, and his testing continued. *Tommy, think about it. Peter even denied the Lord when the Lord needed him most. As a result, he could have seen himself a poster boy for failure. Instead, he met the test, endured the trials, and when the opportunity arrived for him to preach about the Master before thousands of eager listeners on the Day of Pentecost, he declared his testimony and lifted Jesus before the people.*

All the time she was teaching me the basics of living a godly life, my grandmother continued to face enormous tests of her own. As a single parent, who'd already done her required motherly duties, she now found herself raising her mama's boy in industrial Cleveland where she ran businesses by herself, faced the stiff competition of men in a male-dominated world of business by herself, bought and sold real estate and raw land by herself, endured the heartbreak of a rebellious daughter by herself, and suffered the slings and arrows of an everyday life that was not always sunny—by herself. But the testing she endured is what I saw as the primary ingredient in her success. Sometimes my grandmother taught me about life in the things she said and wrote; sometimes I just caught it. Some things are better caught than taught.

Grandma said "think more, complain less"

In one of her editorials, written for her newspaper—her bully pulpit—my grandmother wrote the following about what it means to have an attitude of gratitude:

I find myself perplexed at the attitude that some people take in reference to some humane or kindly act that they receive from the hands of those who have no obligation to act kindly towards them. There are many people who love to help people, not to be seen or heard of, but from their hearts—and many of them never get a grateful word or a "thank you" from these people. But on the other hand, they hear plenty of complaints.

If we just stop to think, we have so much more to be thankful for than to complain of. Complaining becomes a habit just like gratitude or thankfulness or anything else....

The reason Bible students ... enjoy the Book of Psalms is because of the glory of the Psalms of praise, expressing David's thankfulness and gratitude.... I think it would be mighty nice if we checked and double-checked on ourselves, and tried to cultivate the spirit of thankfulness—if we have a spark of it left—and quit complaining.

That was my grandmother. Always thankful, always positive, always persevering, and always meeting the challenges of the day head-on *because she knew both she and I, with the help of a loving God, would win in the end.* During the many years that have followed, the words, prayers, and unfailing love of my grandmother have helped me work through a multitude of my own hurts and hurdles, giving me hope and help when I needed it so desperately. That's because I learned firsthand that God allowed—and still allows—trials, tests, and temptations to meet me on my path because He wants to make me strong, shape my character, and give me a testimony of faith in His goodness that might be worthy of sharing with others. While the rejection I still feel from my parents will always be a fundamental part of my emotional DNA, my grandmother taught me how to redeem my rejection, channel my concerns, harness my hurts, and use these positive emotional responses to build a life, do ministry, and bring honor to Jesus. How grateful I am that Mama knew what she was doing, and that she gave me the head start I needed so much. The first sermon I ever preached was called "Problems Can Be Blessings." The apostle Paul said it this way: "And we know that all things work together for good to them that love God, to them who are the called according to his purpose" (Romans 8:28).

Have the mind of Christ

Perhaps you can relate. That's why I want you to believe in your heart that where there is no pain, there can be no gain. No guts, no glory. Where there is no cross, there will be no crown. No thorns, no throne. To get to it, you must go through it. Your courage comes from facing reality in the strength and power of Jesus' name. Your strength is born from seeing the obstacles that lie before you and asking the wise God, your Heavenly Father, to give you the resolve to see them more as stepping stones. Wishful thinking is a fool's way to stir up courage. But "having the mind of Christ" as you meet your challenges will win the day. So if you're still asking, *Why am I going through this trouble? Why all this pain? Why do difficulties daily dog my steps with no end in sight?* it's because you must endure your tests and tribulations if you are to have a testimony—the end result of a life that understands the reality of life, and of God's great provision for your life. Every obstacle has an opportunity in it. So don't give up on life; you are in it to win it.

I have not said much about the rejection that every African-American endures in America. On top of our personal and family struggles, we have had to endure the rejection and pain that racism brings. I have learned that it is an American reality and tragedy, and it remains a challenge to press your way through the daily indignities and insults we all experience at the hands of white men and women who are racist. I have learned not to obsess over this evil. Instead, I choose to take authority over it by giving it "no place" and fleeing from its presence by changing my environment. There is always more than one store, one hotel, one clerk. I will take my business elsewhere and report the civil rights violation before I let it keep me from realizing my potential. I will not allow racism to absorb my time or energy because it really is not my problem. It is a white problem. I am too blessed to be stressed, and I was taught by my grandmother to stand up for what I believe, but don't stand still. I cannot and will not be distracted by the demons of denial. Every obstacle is an opportunity. Every knock is a boost.

Where there is no cross, there will be no crown.

It's God's promise to you that as you grow stronger in your faith, you will also become braver. You needn't run with the bulls in Pamplona, Spain, or climb the heights of Mount Everest. You need do nothing so dramatic. You just need to take one small step at a time. Be just a *little* braver. Ask God for just a *little* more courage. Your tests and trials will be with you until the day you die, so don't try to solve all your problems. Simply ask a loving Father to help you see them in perspective, understand them, deal with them, risk learning from them, and allow them to be the grist of a testimony only you will be able to share and, in that sharing, minister to others. My friend Bob Schuller would say: "Inch by inch, anything is a cinch."

My grandmother taught me that only those who risk . . . rule!

Roots and wings

My grandmother taught me that only those who risk . . . rule! I would never discover new oceans unless I had the courage to lose sight of the nearby shore. That's why, in her wisdom, she provided me with the twin gifts of *roots* and *wings:* roots deeply planted in God's love, an appreciation for others, and the recognition that I was a child of the King with a mission in life; and wings she knew would set me free and allow me to soar to heights undreamed of. Both gifts set me on a path to freedom. Without roots, I would not have grown beyond the size of a twig; without risk, my life would have little or no emotion, at least not the kind of emotion that stirs the soul, races the heart, and exhilarates the spirit. So let me pass to you what I've come to embrace at this stage of my life. I call them the ten things worth risking:

To love is to risk not being loved in return.

To laugh is to risk appearing the fool.

To weep is to risk appearing sentimental.

To reach out to help someone in need is to risk involvement.

To expose my feelings and vulnerabilities is to risk exposing my true self.

To share my dreams and ideas before crowds is to risk ridicule.

To hope is to risk despair.

To try is to risk failure.

To fly is to risk falling.

To live is to risk dying.

But no test, no testimony; no risk, no real accomplishment; no vision, no victory. Perhaps that's why the Bible demands that we understand *where there is no vision, the people perish* (Proverbs 29:18). My grandmother loved that verse, and I love reading what she wrote about it: "Ideas are what I call creative visions. Haven't you been holding a conversation with somebody and suddenly they will say: 'I have an idea.'... to them it is a vision of reality. I once heard a man say, 'I wish I could carry out my ideas ... but somehow I can't do the job myself.' From the tone of his voice, this man seemed discouraged. But he should not be. If we can promote ideas and someone else has to see that they materialize, it's okay. So, the man who has the idea is the sower—regardless of how the reaping is done. For how can we reap unless we sow?" To which I add, and how will we ever bear a testimony worthy of the name if we fail to accept and respond with inner resolve the challenges set before us? Remember, ideas are either coming *to* you or going *past* you. Ideas, dreams and visions are the language of the Holy Spirit. God is always talking.

Ideas are either coming *to* you or going *past* you. Ideas, dreams and visions are the language of the Holy Spirit. God is always talking.

Grandma was always there for me

My grandmother knew that unless she went through it to get to it—the sometimes *obstacle course* of raising me, loving me, praying over me and with me—she, too, would become a person of limited testimony. She knew that children whose parents fail to respond to the needs of their little ones suffer from a lack of emotional contact. *She would not let that happen to me.* She knew the child who receives little or limited guidance gets into more trouble, by not doing homework, not being fair or honest or showing compassion for others. My grandmother knew that emotional nurturing was as vital as the nourishing food she gave me to eat three times a day. She saw too many other parents "grow away" from spending time with their children, something they did slowly but surely and became accustomed to. *She refused to allow such behavior to rear its ugly head in our relationship.* Although she was not a psychologist, my grandmother knew instinctively that, when asked of their priorities, children would always answer, "I want to spend time with my parents." *That's why she was determined to make the time and take the time to spend time with me.* It was not easy for her, but she never said, thought, or prayed that it would be easy. Without equivocation or hesitation, she just said to my parents, "Give me the boy; I'll raise him. I'll meet Tommy at the station." That's because she knew that when parents become a no-show, they bring irreparable damage to a child's self-esteem.

Who will care for the children?

Because of the love, caring, and discipline that my grandmother poured upon me, my heart has become unusually sensitized, sometimes beyond what I can physically and emotionally bear. My heart goes out to the nearly four million children in our country, according to recent estimates, who are being raised by their grandparents. It's a number that seems to keep growing—up by 20 percent in this decade alone. I think that is a conservative estimate, because many are being raised by grandmothers while they live with their parents. The reasons? They're all around us, and all too familiar—drug abuse, teen pregnancy, divorce, abuse, and abandonment. Still, someone has to look after the children. That's why my emotions are raw and they run high for the hundreds of thousands of "mama's boys" and "mama's girls" who struggle to survive in a world of disposable children; who endure the tests and the trials of childhood and adolescence *without anyone to tell them their pain can become gain, and that their challenges can become a testimony for good and not for evil.*

Why am I so concerned for our castaway children? Because I see them reaping the whirlwind of the *final days*, a reality affirmed in 2 Timothy 3:1, where we are summarily reminded, "In the last days perilous times will come." The Word of God both warns us and encourages us to be aware of what is happening around us and to neutralize the negative forces assaulting our children by bringing them up in the ways of the Lord. However, instead of training our boys and girls in the immutable precepts of our Heavenly Father, we are throwing our hands into the air and waving them like *we just don't care*. Lots of tests, but no testimony. Trouble abounds, but how will it be redeemed? That's why God is calling us to care like we've never cared before. He is demanding that we be aware, and dare to make a difference, particularly in these days when radio and television are throwing garbage into the hearts and minds of our children, and making them think it is emotionally nutritious. It is not. It is poison. It is bile. It is vile. It is filth . . . and our children are paying the price.

**We now have a generation that has
chosen hip-hop over holiness, hell over heaven,
and greed over God.**

Thus, we now have a generation that has chosen hip-hop over holiness, hell over heaven, and greed over God—a situation much like the pilot who admits to his passengers he is desperately lost, but the good news is that "we're making excellent time." We are testing our children to the breaking point; forcing upon young hearts troubles and tribulation their young spirits were never meant to bear. But it will not result in testimony. The Greek word for "perilous" is the same Greek expression used to speak of the raving demoniacs of Gadara in Matthew 8:28; it means "dangerous and savage." The word also suggests the last days will be energized by demons. "And when he was come to the other side into the country of the

Gararenes, there met him two possessed with demons, coming out of the tombs, exceedingly fierce, so that no man might pass by that way" (Matthew 8:28).

Our children are being assaulted by that which is evil, and otherwise responsible adults are doing little or nothing to rescue our best and our brightest. Our democracy is fast becoming depraved, and capitalism is simply materialism. We are neither compassionate nor conservative. We are out of control. A flawed, free enterprise system is creating captives—young and old—as we and they are gutted by greed, bowing to the altar of "things." We throw at young people via video:

- leased limos

- leased Lear jets

- leased cash

- leased ladies

- and leased record companies and offices that have become the devil's workshop to produce videos, films, and music that victimize the minds of children, sabotage their senses, and falsely teach them they can have things without work, sex without responsibility, and a future without faith.

Trials without testimonies

Tests, trials, tribulations, trouble, and turmoil—but no testimony. Nothing is real. Everything comes from a "rent-a-center" mentality. Hear the words of Ezekiel: "It is a small thing to you, O evil generation, that you not only keep the best of the pastures for yourselves, but trample down the rest? That you take the best water for yourselves, and muddy the rest with your feet? All that's left for my flock is what you've trampled down; all they have to drink is water that you've fouled" (Ezekiel 34:18–19, TLB). Many harvests have passed since the prophet wrote those words, but the Word of our God remains true for our twenty-first century lives; and unless we act on its divine directives, we will continue to see our children fight like dogs in the street or in the concert hall, shoot up in penthouses and hallways, abuse women in Central Park, show disrespect for their parents, and be tested as few have ever been—all without a redeeming testimony of God in their lives.

The good news is that into this terrible mix of pain and perdition comes a loving Savior who reminds us that we are the salt of the earth and the light of the world. Jesus tells us that we can make a difference *because He has made a difference in our own lives.* The good news is that the blessings of God will always belong to the man or woman who, filled with the Spirit of Christ, will be wise enough to change his or her mind in the presence of the facts. *The facts are in: our children are being wasted because they are not wanted.* The message to us as adults is, "Whoever heeds correction gains understanding" (Proverbs 15:32, NIV), for whenever we will what *God wills*, we will know our heart is right, as an unknown writer so persuasively reminds us in these words:

> I ASKED GOD to take away my pride, and God said, "No." He said it was not for Him to take away, but for me to give up.
>
> I ASKED GOD to make my handicapped child whole, and God said, "No." He said, "Her spirit is whole; her body is only temporary."
>
> I ASKED GOD to grant me patience, and God said, "No." He said that patience is a by-product of tribulation. It isn't granted; it is earned.
>
> I ASKED GOD to give me happiness, and God said "No." He said He gives blessings; happiness is up to me.
>
> I ASKED GOD to spare my pain, and God said, "No." He said, "Suffering draws you apart from worldly cares and brings you closer to Me."

I ASKED GOD to help me love others as much as He loves me, and God said, "Ah, finally you have the idea."

My dear reader friend, together *let's get the idea* and transform our tests into testimonies as we think of our children first and help them become trophies of God's mercy and grace, not hapless victims of the reality of these perilous last days. Whatever happens to our boys and girls—good or bad—is *our responsibility*. I learned that from my grandmother. After all, I am Mama's boy.

Tommy at 5 years of age

My parents and me in happier days

Mama and her winning smile

My parents and me at college graduation
from St. Louis University

Mom, me, and Mama – somehow I was always in the
middle, and yet I held them together

Mama, Mom and Willie Roberts, my great grandmother
who passed before I was born

My precious family. . .
Thomas III, Christopher, Channing and Beverly. . .
We are all that's left.

Benjy in his first hat, Channing,
Bev and me at Second Christian

Beverly Jean, me, Brian Ferguson, best man,
Mom and Dad at the wedding

Dad baptizing his youngest son, Christopher

Robert Finch, Tom Benjamin, Melvin Finch
the Finchs are childhood friends of Bishop

Bishop Benjamin, Kirk Franklin (gospel
recording artist), and Beverly

Group photo of when Bishop was selected as one of the
recipients of the Morehouse College Distiguished
Preacher's Award (Dr. Benjamin is in the center of photo)

Dr. Benjamin greeting President Jimmy Carter

Bishop greeting President Clinton

Chapter Six

LOVE IS NOT TO BE PAID BACK ...
BUT TO BE PASSED ON

What great thing would you attempt if you knew you would not fail?
Robert H. Schuller

I remember that last tearful good-bye, and I look forward to a joy-packed reunion. That precious memory triggers another: your honest faith—and what a rich faith it is, handed down from your grandmother Lois to your mother Eunice, and now to you!
1 Timothy 1:4-5 (The Message)

n Eugene H. Peterson's translation *The Message*, the provocative words of John 21:15-17 are rendered as follows:

After breakfast, Jesus said to Simon Peter, "Simon, son of John, do you love me more than these?"

"Yes, Master, you know I love you."

Jesus said, "Feed my lambs." He then asked a second time, "Simon, son of John, do you love me?"

"Yes, Master, you know I love you."

Jesus said, "Shepherd my sheep." Then he said it a third time: "Simon, son of John, do you love me?"

Peter was upset that he asked for a third time, "Do you love me?" so he answered, "Master, you know everything there is to know. You've got to know that I love you."

Jesus said, "Feed my sheep ..."

Understanding the question

If you sense that this text from the Apostle John is a familiar one, you are right, because it's a theme as ancient as time itself: friendly and familiar, compassionate and caring. The subject is love, and our Savior attaches such importance to this theme that, to Peter, He belabors the question, *Do you love me?* However, as was often the case throughout his relationship with Jesus, Peter didn't quite get the drift of what the Master was asking. I can see the puzzled expression on Peter's face. *What are You talking about, Master? Come on, now, what kind of a question is that!* Obviously, the Savior wanted more than a perfunctory yes or no to his thrice-asked question, but was not getting what He sought. He was God, so He surely knew Peter loved him—although Peter's love was at best checkered and inconsistent. Still, Jesus hoped Peter would catch the depth and breadth of the question and take it to its logical conclusion.

What *was* Jesus going after? What was He *really* asking? The Lord was simply checking to see if Peter could extend the love he had for his Master and pass it on to others. Jesus wasn't asking to be loved. He wasn't placing demands on Peter to worship Him, bow down to Him, and give up all to follow Him. Peter had already done that—in his own way. On the contrary, Jesus was saying something I never understood until my grandmother made it real clear to me. One day she said, "Tommy, I want you to remember one thing for the rest of your life. *Love is not to be paid back, but to be passed on.*" That's what Jesus was implying when He kept pressing Peter with the same question. Perhaps He hoped Peter would say, *Yes, Lord, I love You, and I'll take Your love to the end of the world. Or, Yes, Master, of course I love You, and You can count on me to take Your message of healing to the sick, the emotionally disturbed, to abandoned children, to parents who are not getting along, and to all others who need Your loving, compassionate touch.*

But I don't want to beat up on Peter too much, because you and I often come up with similar responses when we are asked, "Do you love Jesus?" Well, of course we love Jesus. We go to church, don't we? We send our children to Sunday school, don't we? We give a tenth of our income to the work of the Lord, don't we? Of course we love Jesus. But as my grandmother would say, "Yes, but have you passed on the Savior's love to someone who needs it desperately? Have you done something for others that reflects the heart of the Savior? Have you reached out to a child, as Jesus did, and respected that child, prayed for and over that child, and, because of your love, expected great things from that child?"

Pass it on

I'm afraid most of us would be hard-pressed to answer my grandmother's questions in the affirmative. For the most part, we have not passed on the love of the Savior. Along with a decline in the quality of everything from shoes to clothes to houses and to automobiles, as a nation, we are also suffering a decline in *passing on love to those who need it most.* Modern life has improved our material welfare, but with these advancements has come a deterioration of standards. The hymnist wrote, "Love divine, all loves excelling." Such love has become shallow, superficial, skin-deep, slushy, sleazy, and sensuous. It is love without sacrifice, love without sincerity, love without soul, love without serving, love without saving, love without the Savior, love without listening to our children and to their desperate cries for help.

When love is not passed on, in the name of Jesus Christ, we become inwardly focused, selfish, commandeered by commercialism, and characterized by conspicuous consumption rather than being known as those who quest for the best.

When love is not passed on, in the name of Jesus Christ, we become inwardly focused, selfish, commandeered by commercialism, and characterized by conspicuous consumption rather than being known as those who quest for the best. The result? We become conformed to the deceit of the world instead of being transformed by the renewing of our minds through the power and potential of Jesus Christ. What has happened to love? Where does it come from? What should we do with it? All these questions and their answers are implicit in the dialogue between the Master and an ancient apostle named Simon Peter. During that surreal breakfast beside the lake, Jesus insisted that Peter get the point in triplicate.

Do you love me more than these? Here's the setting for this curious event. Peter, becoming emotional upon hearing John identify Jesus, jumped out of the boat and swam to the shore as fast as he could. Such was Peter's nature: impulsive, headstrong, and determined. He couldn't help being excited. His emotions ran high. Love Jesus? Of course he loved his Master. But it was largely emotional, not spiritual love for the Master— much like those who sign on the dotted line and join the church emotionally, but who fail to make a spiritual decision to serve God through the various avenues of the church that reach out and touch people who need to be loved—love that's passed on.

Others stand before the altar in a life-changing ceremony and pledge their vows—emotionally—but register little or no spiritual commitment to the covenant of marriage. Then, as God gives them children, their lack of commitment to nurturing their offspring in the things of God continues to be their style, and, too often, the children are left to eat alone, pray alone, watch television alone, do their homework alone, and even go to their premature deaths . . . alone.

That's why this dialog between Jesus and Peter is so important. It highlights the difference between passive love and an active commitment to love; between knowing what is worth appreciating and what is worth loving. My grandmother used to say, "Tommy, I want you to remember you can like things, but be sure that you love people and love God because things are not to be loved. You remember that, and it'll keep you straight for the rest of your life." And if Mrs. Marilla Jackson were still alive today, she'd tell you and me the same thing. She'd remind us that some of us have come into relationships, but we've never really defined *love*. We've accepted less than the best. We've chosen carnal love, sensual love, and physical love, when what we really wanted and needed was spiritual love, wholesome love—God's love.

Feed my lambs

Again and again, my grandmother would remind me we needed to realize that all love comes from one Fountain, one Source, and one Creator. She would say, "Your allegiance to that eternal Power will take you away from the theoretical and move you into the practical. Tommy, don't worry about paying me back. Take the love that I have given you and pass it on." Jesus reminds us, *You can't pay Me back for walking the dusty roads of Galilee and teaching you lessons that you could never learn unless I taught you. You cannot pay Me back for being who I am to you. The only thing you can do is feed My lambs, feed My sheep.* He continues His message of compassion by telling us, *I won't be around here much longer, but I want you, for as long as I'm here, to remember that you must pass it on. My love is not to be paid back, but is designed to be passed on. Give it to somebody, save the children, save the babies, save the lambs, save some lost soul.*

Can you and I demonstrate our debt of gratitude to our Master and Lord except by sowing seeds of love? When we sow a seed, it liberates us and puts us on top of the world. Not long ago I was getting my shoes shined at a little shop in Atlanta, and as I sat there, a man sitting next to me was reading a book by J.A. Rogers, *From Superman to Man*—a powerful, 129- page treatise on our African heritage that I'd heard was out of print and difficult to find. I had admired the book for some time, and told the brother next to me that I hoped I could find a place to buy a copy. He told me how much he was enjoying it for the depth of its historical message. Then, when he stepped down from where he was sitting, he turned to me and said, "Brother, it's yours. Keep the book!" I was blessed and thought, *My, how my grandmother would have enjoyed seeing what I just experienced—an act of love from a stranger who knew how to pass it on.*

Giving love freely to others
opens windows of blessings.

Before my new friend could get away, I said, "Brother, let me tell you something: you're in for a major blessing. Not only did you bless me, you blessed the man of God; not only did you bless the man of God, you blessed the Kingdom; and the more you give, the more He's going to give to you. I wonder if you'd give me your name and address because I want to send you my book. It's the least I could do." The message is that when we keep love to ourselves we close doors of opportunity; *giving love freely to others opens windows of blessings.* That's what God is trying to get us to do—to pass it on.

He doesn't want us to talk about how much we love our children. He wants us to take the love He's given us and pour it into their hearts and souls. *Feed the lambs, feed the sheep.* And when I *pass it on*, love opens up my mind, my heart, and my pocketbook. When I plant seeds of love and reap a harvest of compassion, my sole obligation and privilege is to pass it on. Were we granted a thousand or more years of life on earth, you and I could never repay God for what He's done for us. But we can pass that legacy of love and understanding on to the next generation. And who is in greater need of receiving this boundless resource of love than our babies, our adolescents, and our young people! When I wrote the song "Blessed to Be a Blessing," that is exactly what I had in mind.

A breakthrough idea

Today, God is calling us as a nation and as a people to pass on great quantities of Christ's love so that we see babies rescued, children saved, their minds regenerated, respect for their parents reestablished, and a respect for others built into their lives. We're talking about a new idea, a great idea, God's idea. We're talking about feeding the lambs, serving the lambs, and nurturing the lambs. Jesus keeps telling us to pass it on. Three times He told Peter to do it. How many times must He tell you and me?

Earl Graves, publisher of *Black Enterprise* magazine, has said, "No matter where you are in your career or business, there is always something you can do and someone you can help in order to strengthen the entire black community."

As one who serves others in your own special way, do not be weary in well doing, for in due season you will reap *if you faint not* (Galatians 6:9). If you feed His lambs and nourish His sheep, you will reap if you do not grow weary in your efforts. Sometimes you may regard everything you do as one thankless task after another; you may feel that no one cares about you, your commitment, or your contributions. But you are not doing it for others. You are doing it for your Savior, your Lord, your Master, your God. You are feeding His sheep on His behalf, not on the behalf of others. You are planting seeds of goodness and hope in the Garden of God—especially when you plant such seeds in the tender heart of a child. The love you offer and the wonderful acts of compassion you perform will seldom be paid back to you. It's a mystery, but it's also a reality. Therefore, you will be both spiritual and wise simply to pass it on and expect nothing in return—except to know the joy of feeding His lambs.

Here's what I'm learning: the longer we live, the closer we stand to Jesus; and the more we allow His love to permeate our spirit, the more love we will receive in return. Seldom will we receive exactly what we give out, but God will give us more when we pass it on. It may not come back from the person we helped, but it *will* come back. If we give money to help someone in need, our return may not be in dollars but in health, understanding, and even more compassion. Here's the secret: *nothing happens until we take God's mercy and love and pass it on.* That's when the windows of heaven throw themselves open to us. When we start listening to a child who's been separated from his or her parents; when we start giving our time and talent to teach a child to read, to be respectful, and to be thankful, joy will flood our souls. Jesus showed us how to do it. Now He says, *Do as I do. If you love Me, feed My lambs.*

Every day I saw my grandmother *pass it on*.

If we don't, Jesus has little recourse but to tell us, *Don't bother telling Me how much you love Me. I do appreciate the sentiment, but I just want you to feed My lambs.* I caught this theology of thanksgiving and excellency of love from Grandma's loving hands from the day she picked up a confused little five-year-old boy at the Cleveland railroad terminal. Every day I saw my grandmother *pass it on*. When someone in our neighborhood needed money or was desperate for food or lodging, my grandmother took the love she had inside and passed *it on*. When someone needed a tear dried or a shoulder to cry on, my grandmother reached into her great reservoir of compassion and passed it on. And the more she passed it on to others, the more she passed it on to me. Because of what I saw in her life, my life was changed for eternity.

Mama's Boy—out on his own

But she also did something else. When I was thirteen years old, she took me out of Cleveland—out of what is now called the ghetto—and said, "Tommy, I don't really know if I can give you the kind of instruction or blessing that you need at this time of your life. Nor do I know if I can give you the amount of time you will require as you continue to grow and become a young man. I'm a woman, and you need to be around more men. So I'm going to send you to an all-boys private prep school called Tilton School, in Tilton, New Hampshire."

I said, "Where?"

She said, "The State of New Hampshire."

I said, "All boys?"

She said, "All boys and male teachers."

Tilton? Why Tilton? And how did she know so much about this school? Later, I realized she'd been watching one of television's earliest programs, *What's My Line?*, with host John Daly. On that show, he used to talk about a little school called Tilton he had attended. And so, because the celebrated Mr. Daly was a loyal alumnus and chairman of the board at Tilton, I, too, would soon find myself twenty miles north of Concord, New Hampshire, and ninety miles north of Boston, at an all-boys prep school. Here I was, just thirteen years old. I was beginning to want to get to like girls, and my grandmother was going to send me to an all-boys school? God forbid. I went into a mild depression, which my grandmother quickly brought me out of. Before I knew it, grandmother had engaged the services of a driver, and, with my belongings in tow, we drove all the way to Tilton, New Hampshire, from Cleveland, Ohio. When we arrived, I got out of the car, observed my surroundings, and saw myself at a school that was located in a beautiful, rustic, New England setting. The school population was two hundred and the cost was several thousand dollars a year—and that was in 1956! I could not realize Grandma's sacrificial love until many years later.

**Feeling rejected for a second time,
and fearful of feeling all alone in a strange,
new world, I asked, "Why are you doing
this to me, Mama?"**

Feeling rejected for a second time, and fearful of feeling all alone in a strange, new world, I asked, "Why are you doing this to me, Mama?"

"Because I want to save you, Son," she said. "I am not trying to hurt you, but to help you. I'm doing this because I don't want you to fall into the trap that I see so many others fall into. I don't have a husband, and there's not a man in the home. I don't believe a woman can teach a boy to be a man. So I'm gonna sit you here where there are men who will teach you how to be a man."

I said, "Yes, Mama." There we stood there in the doorway of the school, and as she hugged me good-bye, I found myself slowly being separated from my grandmother for the first time in almost eight years. We both wiped at our tears, trying our bravest to bid each other farewell. Here she was, leaving her little Tommy; and there I was, leaving my "mam-maw." I watched her back away; she couldn't turn her back because she knew I had been through that before. Choking through my tears, and barely able to see her, I said, "Mama, I appreciate all that you're doing for me. What can I . . .?"

She stopped in her tracks and said, "Stop. Hold it, Tommy. You cannot ever pay me back, so don't even try. *Remember, love can never be paid back. It has to be passed on.*" She wiped a few more tears, as did I, and I saw her drive away. As the car made a wide turn and vanished from view, my eyes remained red, with streams of water flowing uncontrollably down my cheeks. All I could hear were her words, Love can never be paid back. It has to be passed on. Looking back, it was one of the greatest lessons my grandmother ever taught me. I have tried to live my life that way; sometimes succeeding and sometimes failing, but never without those words: "Love is not to be paid back . . . but to be passed on."

I cannot express in words that sinking feeling I had when I saw that Chrysler New Yorker pull away from Tilton without me in it. Had I been dumped again? What now? Soon my fears faded as this boys' prep school became my new family. Here I was surrounded by male teachers and students. It is said that we need to be careful what we pray for because we will surely get it. My genius grandmother made sure that what I mostly missed I now would receive. I had male teachers, coaches, counselors, and friends. My grandmother had done it again. She did not desert me. She was *developing* me. She saw that as much love as she had in her heart for me, she could not fully make me a man without serious male influence. *Voila!* Tilton School became the father and she remained the mother.

Those were formative and foundational years at Tilton, where a boy became a man. I would visit my grandmother on Christmas and summer breaks. I was still a mama's boy, and she knew it, she loved it, and demonstrated it in so many ways.

I cannot forget the care packages she sent to Tilton by mail. The whole school would wait with tip-toe anticipation for this shoe box wrapped in brown paper that had grease spots on it from the fried chicken and greens inside. Many of my white classmates had never tasted chicken like this and had never had collard and mustard greens mixed. I often had to fight my way into the mailroom and then fight my way out because the aroma had announced the arrival of the mighty chicken for Mama's boy.

My grandmother never stopped giving. I graduated from Tilton with honors and was preparing to go either to Harvard or Boston University, as I had been accepted at both. But my grandmother encouraged me to go to St. Louis University and reconnect with my father. (Throughout my growing-up years I had returned to St. Louis to visit my parents during holidays and summer vacations.) Ultimately that is what I did. It was a blessing as I lived in his home and was a day student at the university. It was quite a transition, but by the grace of God my father and I built a bond.

Every child should somehow, where possible, get to know his or her father. My grandmother had done it again. She put me back together with my estranged father, who had been unprepared to raise me during adolescence. He picked up the baton during my college years and paid all my tuition and expenses. My grandmother taught me to honor my father and mother regardless of the circumstances. She would often say, quoting the Bible: "Honor thy father and thy mother, that thy days may be long upon the land which the LORD thy God giveth thee" (Exodus 20:12). I never did completely understand nor become "one" with my father and mother, but I did honor them. I was probably too much like my father and subconsciously resented my mother, but I did honor them. As the years unfolded, I began not to assign blame because there is always more to it than what is apparent.

Three dates will be forever etched in my memory: 1989, 1990, and 1991. In 1989, my mother died. In 1990, my father died. In 1991, Mama's boy lost his grandmother. For a moment, it seemed as if all of the air had gone out of my balloon and whatever covering I enjoyed was now lifted. I was exposed and exhausted from going to and from the cemetery. And then it hit me again. God is good. You are blessed. Do not complain. Your parents are in heaven. Your grandmother is next to Jesus. You are loved and love is not to be paid back but to be passed on. My spirit leaped. I laughed. Now I am trying to live it out by the grace of God. After all, I am Mama's boy.

God has a "pass it on" plan for you

Every mother and father who reads these words knows what I'm talking about. Sometimes your children don't act the way they should; they don't express the gratitude they ought to show you, and sometimes you wonder whether it was you who even raised them. But here's a word of comfort from a pastor: Hold on. Don't give up. Hang in there. Be not weary in well doing. Your children may never say thank you to you, but if you can just urge them to take the love you've given them and *pass it on*, they won't have to say thank you . . . they'll just give it to your grandchildren and to your great-grandchildren. The good news *is* that God *has* a complete plan for our prosperity. It's called "pass it on". Because the Bible is right: the measure you give is the measure you get (Mark 4:24).

As I look at the calendar on the wall and recall the past goodness of the Lord and the great mercy He's shown me, I recognize I can repay nothing. My ocean of debt is so great and my boat is so small. I cannot repay my Jesus for hanging the sun in the sky, or for placing the stars in their billions of sockets. I can't pay Him back for waking me up this morning and starting me on my way. I can't repay the Lord for the health in my body and the strength in my limbs. I can't pay Him back, but I can feed His sheep. I can feed His lambs. *I can make a difference in the life of a child*. No, I can't pay Him back. I can't pay Jesus back for dying for me. I can't pay Him back for the wounds in His side. I can't pay Him back for the nails in His hands. I can't pay Him back for the crown of thorns so angrily placed on His brow, but I can tell somebody that He lives, and that He can live in any heart that opens up to His love and grace. I can't pay Him back, but I can tell somebody His story—which is inextricably bound to my story—a story that will be my theme in glory. Like the hymnist wrote, "I love to tell the story of unseen things above. . . . 'Twill be my theme in glory—to tell the old, old story of Jesus and His love."

We can't pay Him back, but we can help somebody today as we walk along life's road. As the songwriter has said, "If I can help somebody as I pass along, if I can show somebody they are traveling wrong, then my living shall not be in vain." Love worthy of its name cannot be paid back; it can only be passed on. *Only one life, twill soon be past, and only what's done for Christ will last.* That's why it's both our obligation and our privilege to share the love of Jesus with the next person we meet—to another beggar who, like you and me, is desperately searching for the bread of life. I often tell people that "I am just a blessed beggar trying to tell other beggars where to find some bread."

Feed My lambs, Peter. How much do you really love Me, Peter? A challenging question for Peter—and for you and me. Do we love our Master more than nightclubs, day clubs, service clubs, fraternities, sororities, lodges, football games, basketball games, baseball games, golf, tennis, and TV? Do we love our Lord more than our wife, our husband, our children, our family, and our friends? Those who have eyes to see and ears to hear understand what the Bible means when it says, "Seek ye first the kingdom of God, and his righteousness, and all these things shall be added unto you" (Matthew 6:33). And how are they added? As we wrap ourselves in God's love . . . and then pass it on. For love is not a debt we owe, but a seed that we sow. As we often say in our church: "When I think of the goodness of Jesus and what He has done for me, my soul cries, 'Hallelujah,' for saving a wretch like me."

An ex-convict's lesson in love

In his great novel *Les Miserables*, Victor Hugo tells the story of Jean Valjean, whose only crime was the theft of a loaf of bread to provide food for his sister's starving children. Before finally being turned out penniless on the streets, Valjean had served nineteen years in prison for his "heinous" crime. Now cynical, hardened, and unable to find employment, Valjean finally makes his way to the home of an old Bishop he hopes will help him find his way back into society. The bishop complies by providing the ex-convict with a nourishing supper and a warm bed for the night. But the man of God does more than simply serve the hapless ex-convict; he serves Valjean by setting the table with his very best silver platters and candlesticks, which Valjean quickly recognizes as being of enormous value. Yielding to temptation, Valjean later tucks the costly plates under his arm and slips quietly away from the Bishop's home, only to be caught and returned to the place of the crime by watchful police. When the authorities show the Bishop the stolen silver plates, the good priest says to the policeman, "Why, these are the very silver platters I gave to Valjean. He didn't steal them." Then, turning to the thief, he adds, "And Jean, here, you forgot to take the candlesticks." A stunned and grateful Valjean accepts the candlesticks as more than valuable silver pieces, but as expressions of love beyond measure. The rest of this amazing story details how the Bishop's simple act of kindness—of passing on love, compassion, and forgiveness when he had no reason to do so—brought about true repentance and a changed life.

So I ask you, who can know the great power that may emanate from you and your single act of kindness? You may feel your deed is woefully small, uneventful, and seemingly unimportant. Like the good Bishop, you may even find yourself reframing an injury or an insult and engaging in an act of forgiveness, when harsh justice would seem the more logical course of action. But you choose not to judge. You simply love, understand, and forgive. You decide not to return evil for evil. Instead, you pass on the love that resides in your heart. Suddenly, what seems inconsequential to you becomes a deed of sheer greatness in the eyes and heart of the one in need of love. That's what it means to *pass it on*. It's good to be a child of God and know it; it's better to be a child of God and show it.

Mama's Boy

*My dear Jesus, I can never pay You back, but I can
demonstrate my eternal gratitude to You this day by sowing
seeds of kindness, compassion, and love. Take my heart,
Jesus, my life, and all that I have. Use it for Your glory and
for Your Kingdom. Just now, in the distance, I hear Your
lambs calling—Your precious, young lambs—children who
need to know about You, Your love, and Your salvation. I
want to be faithful to You, so I will follow their voices, heed
Your words, take Your love—and I will pass it on. Because I
know You are infinitely more interested in my walk than in
my talk. Amen.*

Chapter Seven

LOVING OTHERS— GOD'S WAY

*When it comes to love or anything
else, only those who risk ... rule!*
T.G. Benjamin
Boys To Men

*And now abide faith, hope love, these three;
but the greatest of these is love.*
1 Corinthians 13:13 (NKJV)

The book is called *Letters to an Unborn Child*, the story of David Ireland and the heartbreak he writes about in thirteen short epistles to a child he will never meet. Suffering from a disease that will take his life before his child is born, Ireland pours his heart and soul into a tape recorder, words that were later transcribed and printed in one of the most moving books on unconditional love anyone could ever read. Because he will soon die, this loving father will never be able to take his child on piggyback rides, go to birthday parties, or do the wonderful, simple things a father is blessed to do. Instead, he does all he knows how to do: write a few letters through which his child will be able to know him.

As you read this brief excerpt from his treatise on love and compassion, realize that Ireland is wheelchair-bound and must be fully reliant on his precious wife, Joyce, for everything. The words he speaks are for the child he will never hold or be able to love. David Ireland says,

> Your mother is very special. Few men know what it's like to receive appreciation for taking their wives out to dinner when it entails what it does for us. It means that she has to dress me, shave me, brush my teeth, comb my hair, wheel

me out of the house and down the steps, open the garage and put me in the car, take the pedals off the chair, stand me up, sit me in the seat of the car, twist me around so that I'm comfortable, fold the wheelchair, put it in the car, go around to the other side of the car, start it up, back it out, get out of the car, pull the garage door down, get back into the car, and drive off to the restaurant. And then, it starts all over again: she gets out of the car, unfolds the wheelchair, opens the door, spins me around, stands me up, seats me in the wheelchair, pushes the pedals out, closes and locks the car, wheels me into the restaurant, then takes the pedals off the wheelchair so I won't be uncomfortable. We sit down to have dinner, and she feeds me throughout the entire meal. And when it's over she pays the bill, pushes the wheelchair out to the car again, and reverses the same routine.

And when it's all over—finished—with real warmth she'll say, "Honey, thank you for taking me out to dinner." I never quite know what to answer.[1]

God's definition of love

What a story of unconditional love—and I have only shared with you a brief segment of this book, which page after page speaks of this amazing love, a God-given love. The kind of love the apostle writes about in 1 Corinthians 13. Love that never quits. Love that doesn't think more highly of itself than it should. Love that doesn't behave rudely. Love that doesn't demand the spotlight. Love that doesn't envy the accomplishments of others. Love that believes . . . hopes . . . and endures. The kind of love that takes you and me beyond ourselves. It reminds us *we can give without loving,* but *we can never love without giving.* It is a kind of love that we will never be able to demonstrate in our own strength. That's because this love is Jesus love, God love. The Greek word for this unconditional pos-

---

[1] David Ireland with Louis B. Tharp Jr. *Letters to an Unborn Child* (New York, Evanston, San Francisco, London: Harper & Row Publishers, 1974), pp. 33–34.

itive regard is *agape*—an undefeatable attitude of goodwill toward others. It means that no matter what another person does to you and me, we will never, under any circumstances, seek anything but that person's good. Would you agree with me that our world needs this kind of love, the Savior's love?

**We can give without loving,
but we can never love without giving.**

So what is love?

It is silence—when your words can hurt.

It is patience—when your neighbor's curt.

It is deafness—when a scandal flows.

It is thoughtfulness—for other's woes.

It is promptness—when stern duty calls.

It is courage—when misfortune falls.

This is the kind of love I grew up with once my parents sent me to live with my grandmother. From day one, all I knew was love. With her life, my grandmother echoed the words of Martin Luther King Jr., who said, "I've decided to stick with love. Hate is too great a burden to bear." She knew that indifference and not caring were the strongest enemies of love. She lived Ephesians 4:29, and she made sure I heard the apostle Paul's message loud and clear: "Do not let any unwholesome talk come out of your mouths, but only what is helpful for building others up according to their needs, that it may benefit those who listen" (NIV). Oh, how she loved me.

Mama loved me so much that she also gave me my share of spankings, using her hand or whatever was handy to get her point across. In retrospect, it was not abuse but a blessing. I can remember one day, as an expression of her unconditional love, combined with conditioned frustration, she even threw a couple of shoes at me—just to get my attention. If I would pout and drop my lip in disgust, her response would not be verbal. She would simply reconstruct my mouth with one swift backhand, as only she could do. Talking to me or sending me to my room without supper would not have tamed my rebellious spirit. I needed her discipline, which was the basis of her unconditional tough love—although it hardly seemed like love at the time. As I reflect on how my grandmother raised me—and when I see our relationship in respect to the direction many parents are taking their children today—it saddens me to see that we've bought into Dr. Spock, the age of rock and hip-hop. We have lost one generation of our children to drugs, violence, and greed. We are now beginning to lose a second generation. Dr. Spock's *permissive parenting* philosophy has not reformed parenting but deformed it. What may have seemed like love has been the furthest thing from love. To coddle, cajole, and kowtow before our children in fear is not love. Its results are Columbinesque. If anything, it is the foundation for familial rebellion, and rebellion is what we've got. This "stinking thinking" was inadequate for twentieth-century child rearing, and it will be no more useful as we work our way through the twenty-first century. I can only imagine how a dialog between Dr. Spock and Mrs. Jackson might have unfolded. I know I would have felt sorry for the good doctor.

The fun factor

Love has many facets. My grandmother expressed her love for me in so many ways, and one of her most amazing qualities was her gift of humor. She was the funniest woman you could ever meet, a natural-born comedienne. I remember how I'd get in the car with her and say, "Mama, now where are we going?" She'd turn to me with her big, broad smile and say, "We just riding, Jack. We just riding." And then she'd laugh. My, how she could laugh. She laughed so hard that she made me laugh. And once we both got started laughing neither of us could stop. Then, before we knew it, our convulsive laughter turned into tears. On more than one occasion she would laugh so hard that she had to hold her stomach in pain, and say, "Oh, Tommy, I've got to go to the bathroom!" I was catching what love was all about as she cherished me with her laughter, her good humor, and by just being herself.

Grandma and I developed the most affectionate, unique way of saying good-bye in our neighborhood.

And the fun continued, as Grandma and I developed the most affectionate, unique way of saying good-bye in our neighborhood. If I was leaving the house for any period of time, she would position herself in the doorway, stick one foot way out of the door, and then take her two hands and wave them in the air at me. I could only see her hands and legs. It must have been the strangest sight to our neighbors, but it was a unique signal between us that meant, "I love you, Tommy. I love you like nobody else in the world can love you. Now you be careful, you hear?" I don't know exactly how we started engaging in this "good-bye behavior," but it's something she always did. If she was busy, ever forgot her little farewell routine, or just said, "Tommy, be careful," I'd stop in my tracks, look at her for a minute, and wait for her to laugh—and stick her foot out the door and wave to me with both hands high in the air.

Are you all right?

In the summer between Tilton and St. Louis University, I, at seventeen, was driving my grandmother's new Chrysler Imperial and got no further than the corner of my street at Brainard Road and Chagrin Boulevard in the Woodmere suburb of Cleveland. As I drove on Brainard toward the corner of Brainard and Chagrin, I was feeling like a million in this fine new car. I couldn't wait to "show off" this car with me behind the wheel. I approached the stop sign and stopped. I looked to my left and then to my right. It looked clear, but somehow a car appeared on my right as I pulled out and hit the car broadside. Here I was four doors from my house in big trouble. The police and the ambulance came as the passengers in the other car complained of minor injuries.

I was not physically hurt, but emotionally I was a wreck. I was crying. Yes, at seventeen I was crying as I walked back to my grandmother's beautiful ranch home that she built from the ground up with swimming pool and all. Somehow all of this meant little as I knew I had to face her without her brand-new, towed-away automobile. I walked sheepishly up to my front door and rang the bell. When the door opened, she could see my tears and my fears. "Tommy, what happened?" she asked. I told her about the accident and closed my eyes, expecting the worst. Instead, like her words at that train platform when I was five years old, she said, "How's Mama's boy? Are you all right? I don't care about the car. We can get another one of those, but I can't replace you." She hugged me and once again anointed me with unconditional love.

Dr. Karl Menninger, noted doctor and psychologist, was searching for the cause of many of his patients' ills. One day he called in his clinical staff and proceeded to unfold a plan for developing, in his clinic, an atmosphere of creative, unconditional love. All patients were to be given large quantities of love; no unloving attitudes were to be displayed in the presence of the patients, and all nurses and doctors were to go about their work in and out of the various rooms with a loving attitude. At the end of six months, the time spent by patients in the institution was cut in half. My grandmother could have taught the course and even trained the staff in the fine art of unconditional loving.

For as long as I can remember, I was always on the receiving end of practical, helpful, loving advice—because she loved me unconditionally. She was consistent and persistent—

because she loved me unconditionally. (Once my grandmother would get on me about something, I knew it would either break or make me—*because she loved me unconditionally.*) She would look me in the eye and say, "Tommy, if you will be a good boy, you'll be a good man." Real simple, but very accurate. She'd then follow up with, "If you will learn how to be obedient as a boy, it will prove itself to be your direction as a man." She helped me understand that there are no bad boys, only bad choices. There are no bad boys, just misdirected, misused, unloved, unprotected, undisciplined boys who later become misdirected, misused, unloved, unprotected, and undisciplined adults. Day after day my grandmother reminded me there was nothing I could do to make God love me more; happily, there was also nothing I could do to make God love me less. I learned early on that God's love is unconditional, impartial, everlasting, and perfect in every way.

I will be forever blessed because what I received from my grandmother was all I knew. I had no options. My parents were no longer a serious influence in my life; our neighbors were loving collaborators on my behalf, and I dared not disagree with my grandma, for fear of dire consequences. It was just Grandma and Tommy. Whether I appreciated her advice or not, I heard it, took it in, and accepted it.

If she were alive today, and if you asked her, "Mrs. Jackson, what kind of boy was Tommy?" all she would say to you would be, "Tommy was a good boy, and he never gave me any trouble." She meant I learned to stay within my boundaries—not that she didn't get after me, not that I didn't get corrected by the rod, and not that she didn't discipline me, but that I never created the kinds of problems for her that my mother created. My grandmother's boundless love for me—with no conditions—paid off when I was a child, and it continues to make its indelible mark on me every day. I can only imagine my greatest gift to this great woman was that I made her proud and not ashamed.

You can do it!

Growing up, I often got the impression my grandmother felt she'd failed with her daughter *but that she would win with me.* She gave herself a second chance at raising a child, and I was fortunate to be in the right place, at the right time, with the right grandmother to love me. And she did it all alone— just as so many single mothers and grandmothers today must bear the responsibility of raising a child or a grandchild alone. If you are such a person, I hope you know how much my heart goes out to you. At the same time, I would also like to debunk the myth that says *you can't do it alone.* I know it's tough. I know at times it may seem hopeless—especially with the social, school, and street pressures that are coming down on the children you love. But *to raise a child alone is not impossible*—not if you take the time, make the time, and use the time to pour your unconditional love into your child.

To raise a child alone is not impossible.

There does come a time, however, when a woman cannot adequately raise a boy to be a man, not by herself. Because a woman has never been a man, she cannot teach what she does not know. This is where you can be wise—even as my grandmother was wise—by engaging the help of male mentors, coaches, pastors, youth leaders, members of the community, and next-door neighbors. On Bryant Avenue, my grandmother, by her actions, admitted she could not raise me adequately by herself. She would say to our neighbor, "Mr. Caldwell, would you please teach my Tommy how to fish? Will you be his fishing teacher, his fishing mentor, his fishing buddy, and his fishing father?" What do you think Mr. Caldwell said? He said, "Tommy, let's go fishing for two days over in Sandusky. What do you say to that?" I said, "When do we leave?" Grandma just smiled approvingly, and thanked a gracious Mr. Caldwell for participating in loving a little boy unconditionally and helping him to grow up to become a good man. I'm sure in heaven Mama has thanked Mr. Caldwell many times, and one day I will too.

Grandma loved me so much that she brought as many people as possible into our family circle and encouraged them to influence me and help me grow mentally, socially, and spiritually. Over time, I realized that grandma had this little pact going with our neighbors. Sam taught me how to swim. Even though I almost drowned with his help, Sam did his best. God bless Miles Turner, who taught me the value of hard work. Mr. Jones, by his kindly actions, gave me clues on what it means to be a responsible father. I remember he and his wife had three children, but they were never too busy to take me in as one of their own.

**If you are a single parent,
doing the hard work of raising your
children alone, you must not live under
condemnation because you are going solo.
You are not a second-class person because you are
doing your best *alone*, regardless of
the reasons for *being* alone.**

Why am I telling you all this? Because if you are a single parent, doing the hard work of raising your children alone, you must not live under condemnation because you are going solo. You are not a second-class person because you are doing your best *alone*, regardless of the reasons for *being* alone. I want you to recognize that you have the God-given potential and power to love your child and meet the physical, spiritual, and social needs of your child by inviting others to help stand in the gap—to help you do the things you feel you cannot do. Yes, it does take a village to raise a child—especially for a single parent. The good news is that it's still possible to raise a child with integrity, with good values, and with a love for

Jesus—and to love your child unconditionally. And when you ask others to help you in your struggle, it can make all the difference in a child's life, just as it made all the difference in mine. I wish I could list the number of outstanding persons who were raised by a single parent or particularly by a grandma like I had.

Tap into the willing universe of people who would be more than pleased if you asked them to be included and involved in helping you to raise your child successfully. Ask and you shall receive. God will honor your request. He will prepare the hearts of more people than you can imagine who are willing to be a Sam, a Mr. and Mrs. Jones, or a Mr. Caldwell for your precious little boy or girl. Find out who they are. Let them know you need them to love your little ones. Give them the privilege of pouring their own brand of unconditional love into the heart and soul of your child. Yes, unconditional love has its risks, but only those who risk . . . rule. The results are worth the risk, in Jesus' name.

A boy loved the Babe unconditionally

One of the all-time greats in baseball was Babe Ruth. His bat had the power of a cannon, and his record 714 home runs remained unbroken until Hank Aaron came along with his own firepower. The Babe was the idol of sports fans, but age took its toll, and his popularity began to fade. Finally the Yankees traded him to the Braves.

In one of his last games in Cincinnati, Babe Ruth began to weaken. He struck out and made several misplays that allowed the Reds to score five runs in one inning. As the Babe walked toward the dugout, chin down and dejected, there rose from the stands a chorus of boos and catcalls. Some fans shook their fists—a sight the Babe had not often seen in his great career.

Then a wonderful thing happened. A little boy jumped over

the railing, and with tears streaming down his cheeks he ran out to the great athlete. Unashamedly, he flung his arms around the Babe's legs and held on tightly. Babe Ruth scooped him up, hugged him, and set him down again. Patting him gently on the head, he took his hand and the two of them walked off the field together. There it was: *love completely without conditions.* The boy loved his hero just for who he was—win, lose, hit, or strikeout. It didn't matter to the boy, and it shouldn't matter to us.

When Jesus was carrying out His earthly ministry, He was underrated, misunderstood, attacked, and maligned. Why? Because He took the risk to take dead aim at centuries-old dead traditions and laws that no longer served any practical purpose. What had once been important theological glue for Jewish society had now become an oppressive yoke around the necks of the children of Israel. Here's how it looked.

In contrast to the two commands of Christ, the Pharisees had developed a system of 613 laws and 365 negative commands. By the time Christ came to preach, teach, and heal, the system had produced a heartless, cold, and arrogant brand of righteousness. As such, it contained at least ten tragic flaws—perhaps more:

1. New laws had to be constantly invented for new situations.

2. Accountability to a loving Heavenly Father was replaced by accountability to rigid, intractable men.

3. The laws reduced a person's ability to discern good from evil.

4. They created a judgmental spirit in the hearts of people.

5. The law-lovers confused personal preferences with divine law.

6. The laws produced inconsistencies that were difficult to live with.

7. They created a false standard of righteousness.

8. They became a terrible burden to the Jews.

9. They were strictly external, giving no comfort to internal needs or struggles.

10. They were ultimately rejected by Jesus.

Living by the cross

How different was Jesus' approach! His love was kind, unconditional, open, freedom-giving, and attractive. Yet, Jesus did not take suffering lightly. The good news was that He provided—and continues to provide—strength for our daily needs when we most need His loving touch. A friend recently sent me some words of encouragement on the importance of living by the cross of Jesus Christ and by faith in our Heavenly Father's promises. These words of comfort speak to my own heart as I continue to struggle with my own challenges—just as the twists and turns of your life demand that you struggle with yours. This person writes,

We have crosses to bear every day. But I have learned to enjoy the bitterest of them. And it is sweet to know that the heaviest cross can be borne in peace. However, there may be times when it seems that you do not have the strength even to bear it or to drag it. All you can do is fall down beneath it, overwhelmed and exhausted. I pray that God may spare you as much as possible in proportioning your suffering, not that God delights in seeing us suffer, but He knows that we need this as much as we need our daily bread. And only God knows how much we need to accomplish His purposes in our lives. The words of the hymn are still true: "Must Jesus bear the cross alone and all the whole world go free? No, there's a cross for every one, and there's a cross for me." We should always remember the truth of 1 Corinthians 10:13:

"There hath no temptation taken you but such as is common to man; but God is faithful, who will not permit you to be tempted above that ye are able, but will, with the temptation, also make the way to escape, that ye may be able to bear it."

So what we must do is live by faith and live by the cross. For we are confident that God, with His true compassion, proportions our trials to the amount of strength that He has committed to us within. Even though we cannot actually see this happening, yet we believe it is true. Trial and strength are portioned out in equal measure. Living by this kind of faith demands our deepest kind of death to self.

We serve a loving, merciful God who wants the best for you and for me. But pain is part of our life's work: *the surest way to remain unhappy is to keep our hurt inside.* God wants us to enjoy the best of both mental and spiritual health. The secret to true health is to tell others who hurt you that they hurt you *when* they hurt you. Hurt is the pain of the moment. Fear, trouble, and anxiety are pain in the future.

The secret to true health is to tell others who hurt you that they hurt you *when* they hurt you. Hurt is the pain of the moment. Fear, trouble, and anxiety are pain in the future.

As children of God, we believe that the truth of Jesus Christ will set us free—now and forever. This freedom that would be ours comes only from a spirit of openness and a desire to grow; for only the open, the vulnerable, and those willing to admit they do not have all the answers are truly free.

Jesus Christ keeps telling us that it takes only a minute or two to do it right. When we rush off in all directions and determine to carve our own paths, we lose our balance and forget our purpose—which is to love God and to enjoy Him forever. Unlike the song of the sixties, the answer is not blowing in the wind. The answers to our greatest challenges—our need for love without conditions, our cries for mercy in raising our children, and our pleas to help us make ends meet when darkness and pain surround us—can all be found in the loving heart of our Heavenly Father and His beloved Son, Jesus Christ.

My grandmother taught me that when we look at our defects through the eyes of Jesus, they vanish before His glory and love. She also taught me that when we focus on our blemishes and on our inability to get things right—forgetting that Jesus loves us, and that He has a wonderful plan for our life—we become restless, anxious, and interrupt the flow of God's unconditional love for us. Neither you nor I understand why our lives take the directions they do. We can hazard guesses, but they are only guesses. We may not know what the future holds, but one thing we can know for certain, *we know the One who holds the future—our future—whether we understand it or not.* For . . .

Not until each loom is silent

And the shuttles cease to fly,

Will God unroll the pattern and explain the reason why

The dark threads are as needful in the weaver's skillful hand

As the threads of gold and silver

For the pattern which is planned.

A Hasidic parable tells the story of a hungry boy who was hiking through the forest with his father. Suddenly the boy spotted a berry patch and began eating. The hour was late, but the boy was so hungry that he could not stop eating. The father said, "I will start out, and you may stay a few minutes longer. But to avoid getting separated, I want you to keep calling, *Father, Father!* When I hear you, I will answer you. However, when my voice begins to fade, come running to me as fast as you can." We must keep our children close enough to the Father to always hear His voice.

If we are to stay in touch with the unconditional love of the One who lived, died, and rose again to bring us freedom, we had best not stay too long at the berry patch—but, instead, keep calling, "Father, Father." For when He hears us, He will answer. But whenever His voice starts to fade, let us go running to Him as fast as we can. And as you and I go running, sometimes we will need a few tips, some practical advice, on how best to express our love. Let me share some of these with you. Try them in your own life. I think you'll agree they'll help you take what may be a dull day and turn it into something spectacular.

Ten ways to say "I Love You"

What do you give when his dresser is full of cologne and you're both on diets? When she thinks flowers die too soon, and you've already spent next month's paycheck? And when your child has all the latest toys and computer gadgets and is already bored with what he or she sees in the store window? Here are ten inexpensive ways to share your unconditional love with the one—and the ones—you love.

1. Send a love letter listing the reasons "Why I love you so much."

2. Plan a surprise lunch, complete with picnic basket, sparkling grape juice, and goblets.

3. Kidnap the car for a thorough washing and detailing.

4. Compose a love song and sing it.

5. Arrange for someone to sing a favorite love song to you and your love when you're together.

6. Call a radio station and have them announce a love message from you and make sure your loved one is lis-

tening at the right time.

7. Hide love notes in the car, a coat pocket, or desk, or in a school lunch bucket.

8. Florist flowers aren't the only way to say, "I love you." Pluck a single flower and write a message about how its beauty reminds you of your love. For even greater impact, have it delivered at work.

9. Prepare a surprise candlelit, gourmet, low-calorie dinner for you and the ones you love. The act will outshine the taste.

10. Promise to change a habit that someone you love has wanted you to change.

My grandmother would have especially liked number ten: Promise to change a habit that someone you love has wanted you to change. She was after me all the time about this—and I was able to do it easier than many because I saw consistent modeling every day from someone I loved. Grandma taught this Mama's boy there was great mutual reward if I would express an attitude of love to everyone I would meet. She wrote about this in one of her many editorials:

> I believe that no evil comes out of good ... that peace is greater than all riches—if you will recognize peace when it comes to you ... that love begets love ... that two wrongs can't make a right—even though at times revenge does seem sweet ... that kindness to one's fellowman is essential to living ... that a smile is contagious ... and a hearty laugh cures minor ills.

The ever-positive, affirming, uplifting Mrs. Jackson would have loved to meet my friend and brother Dennis Kimbro, who writes in a similar vein:

> We increase in value whatever we praise. The entire universe responds to praise.... Children glow with joy and gladness when they are praised by parents and loved

ones. Even the plant world grows fuller and healthier for those who praise and nurture it. We can praise our own ability and in turn expand and increase our potential as we speak words of encouragement. Whatever we increase in potential increases in value. The unfailing law of increase is, whatever is praised and blessed multiplies.

The Creator gave you dominion over the earth. Count your blessings and they, too, will increase. Everything is your servant. If you are working for someone else and you desire a better job or more pay, start by blessing and being thankful for the job you have. Bless your current line of work; be thankful for every opportunity it gives you to acquire greater skill and the ability to serve others. Bless the money you earn, no matter how little it may be. Be thankful for the opportunity to serve faithfully, no matter how small the immediate reward. Give your best, give it cheerfully, gladly, thankfully, and you will be amazed how quickly your increase will come.[2]

How could anyone say it better? Now the question is, how about you? Are you persuaded that the unconditional love of Jesus can make a difference in your life? Do you believe it can help you do a better job of loving your spouse and raising your child? Will you take the words of my grandmother to heart— "that love begets love ... that two wrongs don't make a right— even though at times revenge does seem sweet ... that compassion, kindness to one's fellowman is essential to living"—and make them part of your relational DNA? I hope so. I also hope you'll remember that there's great power in one—in one idea, in one person, in one act of kindness, in a loving single parent, in a loving couple, and in the One who loves us, died for us, rose for us, and lives in our hearts so that we may live as we were created to be—free from bondage, free to love, and free to be conformed to the image of our Savior and Lord Jesus Christ.

---

[2] Dennis Kimbro, *Daily Motivations for African-American Success* (New York: Faucett Columbine, 1993), April 28.

The Color of My Eyes

As told by my friend, Bishop J. D. Wiley

New Orleans, LA

I was watching a movie one time and this guy met this girl in a bar. He was smooth and he was trying to pick her up, telling her all the good things. All of a sudden she looked down toward the floor and said, "Would you like to take me out?"

The look on his face said, *I've scored!*

"Dinner, dancing, go to my place, nightcap?" He was smiling from ear to ear as if to say, *conquered again.*

She said, "Before we go, do you think I'm attractive?"

"Yeah."

She is looking at the floor. "Before we go, tell me the *color of my eyes.*

The brother was dumbfounded.

She went on to say, "You want to sleep with me, you want to make love, but you don't know what color my eyes are."

Often times the Lord says, "You want Me to bless you with ministries and dreams and husbands and wives and cars, but what color are My eyes?"

We too often come before God seeking His hands and not His face.

Chapter Eight

OUR CHILDREN: A PRIORITY, NOT A PROGRAM

When you save a boy, you save a man.
When you save a man, you save a marriage.
When you save a marriage, you save a family.
When you save a family, you save your community.
Save our boys.
T. G. Benjamin
Boys To Men

Be not deceived, God is not mocked, for whatsoever
a man soweth, that shall he also reap.
Galatians 6:7(KJV)

The great African-American educator Dr. Benjamin Mays, former president of Morehouse College, reminded each of us of our need to place great value on time when he said:
We only have a minute.

There are 60 seconds in it.

Didn't choose it, can't refuse it.

But it is up to me to use it.

I must suffer if I abuse it.

Give account if I lose it.

We only have a minute,

but eternity is in it.

The lowly minute. Those seemingly unimportant sixty seconds. But what awesome power lies within that unit of time, which, when multiplied over an hour, a day, a week, a month, a year—a life—becomes the very stuff of our existence. Those individual sixty seconds are also the only resource we possess with which to love our children, educate them in heart and mind, lead by example, tell them they're special miracles from God, remind them they have a unique place in our world, and that we will always give them priority in our lives and not relegate them to being just part of a program.

If you and I want to become depressed, all we have to do is consider the formidable challenges of child raising—and how so many mothers and fathers have turned over their parental responsibilities to schools, clubs, coaches, after-school sports, the TV, and other programs. If we want to become even more discouraged, we need only to look around to see the thousands of innocent children who are parental throwaways, boys and girls who are still standing alone on their own lonely railroad platforms *with no one showing up to pick them out and pick them up.* If we want to throw in the towel even more quickly, we simply need to focus on the millions of children who are at risk because of their parents' divorce, unfaithfulness to each other, their drive for material possessions, workaholicism, or other heartbreaking reasons. Our best and our brightest are being thrown on the rocks and cannibalized by a media that does not care about values, and a society at-large that has other priorities—few of which includes the emotional, physical and spiritual health of our nation's children.

Every knock is a boost

My grandmother knew what was happening in her time, and if she were alive, she'd be just as savvy about what's going on today with parents and children. She was a student of people, of society, and of the interaction between children and their parents. She was also an overcomer and forever determined to prove the statistics wrong. With her can-do attitude, she provided hope and encouragement to single parents and grandparents when she was alive; now, long after her death, her legacy lives in my heart and in the hearts of thousands who've been impacted by her faith in God, her life of prayer, and her commitment to do whatever was necessary to make children a priority and not rely on programs to raise them. And I was the recipient of all of that love.

**My grandmother said, "Remember,
they picked on Jesus. *They'll also pick on you.*"**

She would often tell me, "Tommy, life's not going to be easy. But remember, every knock is a boost. You are going through what you're going through because God is developing you into that person He created you to be. Remember, they picked on Jesus. *They'll also pick on you.*" Imagine what it's like to live with that kind of honesty day after day. No wonder I felt special. No wonder I felt I was a priority when my grandmother would hold up a Bible and say, "Tommy, what does this Book say about that? Come on, what does it say? What does God say? I'll tell you what He says . . . *That I can do all things through Christ who strengthens me.* Either you can do it or you can't. Jesus didn't say you can't. He said you can. Success comes in cans. I can. I can. I can." Those daily, weekly—sometimes hourly—sermonettes took hold in my young heart and became the foundation of my life and ministry.

What would our children be like today if parents and grandparents took a page from my grandmother's playbook on child raising and made their children the priority they deserve? Do you think there would be as much youth crime? As much young adult cynicism? As much sorrow and defeatism? I don't think so.

Mama would not only speak her mind, but she would deliver her message evangelically and boldly. Never reticent to give good reason for the hope that lived within her, she didn't have a timid bone in her tiny body. She'd fight, debate, and argue her point of view. She'd often say, *There's only one life, twill soon be past, only what's done for Christ will last.* She loved Jesus, she loved children, and she loved me. She also knew that adults needed to be encouraged by the faith of children—just as the little ones brought such great encouragement to Jesus. She'd remind me of how the children who lined the streets and lanes must have made Jesus smile as He rode on a borrowed colt into Jerusalem and entered the temple on His day of triumph. Children of all ages waved palm branches and sang, "Hosanna to the Son of David" (Matthew 21:15). She made the scene come alive for me—and, in the process, helped me understand the heart of Jesus. Grandma knew when adults are taken down by trouble and despair that they, too, need to surround themselves with the life and laughter of children, spend time with their little ones, learn from their simple faith, and see their own lives through the honest eyes of those in their care.

I remember my grandmother telling me often her time on earth would soon come to an end, and that I would not be able to rely on her forever. Relatively speaking, she was right: *she lived in the shadow of death, but she feared no evil.* In fact, there were times when I feared for her life—she was that fearless, determined, and resolute. I will never forget one summer Saturday morning. I had just awakened at around eight o'clock. I was thirteen years old, and we were now living in the hotel grandma owned and named after me, the Hotel Thomas. That morning I heard a tremendous commotion in front of the hotel, but I wasn't able to determine what was going on. I just knew people were scurrying about, yelling, shouting, and that everything was in a general state of confusion.

By the time I threw on some clothes and got to the front porch, I couldn't believe my eyes: there was my little five-foot-tall grandmother engaged in a fist fight with a man more than six feet, weighing about two hundred pounds. She was up at his chest, beating him with her fists as if he were a drum. He looked down at her; she looked up at him, and they just continued to go at it. Later, I learned that grandma had told this man on several occasions not to park his car in the loading zone of the hotel, because it interfered with the daily deliveries. Oblivious to her demands and, unfortunately for him, unaware with whom he was dealing, he ignored the protests from my grandmother and continued to park in the restricted area. That's when Mrs. Marilla Jackson decided she'd best take the conversation to another level. She forgot about turning the other the cheek. Fortunately, another friend of our family stepped in forcefully and ended the early morning fiasco. I don't think the man ever parked there again.

Grandmother was never confused about her priorities; she demanded and earned respect from everyone. Yet, with all that she had going on in her busy life, she managed to make time for Mama's boy, and she made sure it was always one-on-one.

**"Our boys and girls need life rafts
and life preservers, but mostly they need
stay-at-home parents who are willing to get
into the water with them and rescue them
before it is too late."**

In my earlier book *The Home Alone Syndrome*, I wrote what I still know to be true today, that "this is not the hour to wade timidly into the shallow waters where we pretend things are just fine! . . . things are *not* just fine. The waves are high and our ships are in danger of sinking. We must not stand idly by shouting encouragement to our children from the shore. Our boys and girls need life rafts and life preservers, but mostly they need stay-at-home parents who are willing to get into the water with them and rescue them before it is too late. We must act and *we must act now*. Tomorrow is too late. I hurt for our children and I hurt bad.

• I hurt for children who are left *home alone*.

- I hurt for children whose closest companion is the phone.

- I hurt for little black boys and girls who think that day care is the best care they can receive.

- I hurt for little black boys and girls who call the baby-sitter Mama and the pizza deliveryman Daddy.

- I hurt for children whose primary exercise is working the remote control and whose primary teacher is the television.

- I hurt for children who must decide each day whether they will treat their house as a hotel for sin or as a haven in the time of storm.

- I hurt for kids who get into guns before they get into God.

- I hurt for kids who get into crack before they get into Christ.

My grandmother could just have easily written those words—because she also hurt when she saw how children were not receiving the love, training, one-on-one companionship, and loving parental acceptance so critical to a child's emotional, social, and spiritual growth. She understood the wisdom of Galatians 6:7: "Be not deceived, God is not mocked, for whatsoever a man soweth, that shall he also reap." In the language of the street, she would have said, *What goes around comes around,* or, *Every dirty deal has a two-way ticket*.

Years later I found myself preaching, teaching, and writing what I learned at my grandmother's knee:

If you have to choose between saving your child and getting a new coat—*save your child*. If you have to choose between saving your child and getting a new car—*save your child*. If you have to choose between saving your child and going on a cruise—*save your child*. If you have to choose between saving your child and buying a new home—save your child. Our children must be a priority, not relegated to a program run by others, as well meaning as those programs may be. That's because your child does not want your things. Your child wants YOU— and YOU come in those seemingly insignificant sixty-second units. When your children know you are making them a priority, their self-esteem skyrockets; satisfaction with their smallest skills pushes through previous pain; they no longer settle for second best; fear and failure are no longer viable options.

Seven ways to be a better parent

How will you as a parent achieve these kinds of results from your children? In at least seven ways:

1. Stay home more and step out less.

2. Work on your problems instead of worrying about them. Recognize that every problem is a platform for a miracle in your child's life.

3. Pray for and with your child every day.

4. Believe that when God gives you unparalled trials, He also promises to provide unparalled triumphs.

5. Accept the fact that *attitude* is the only difference between success and failure.

6. Bend your child toward the Person of Jesus Christ. "Train up a child in the way he should go and, when he is old, he will not depart from it" (Proverbs 22:6).

7. Don't send your child to church—take him.

Bend your child toward the Person of Jesus Christ.

There will always be tension between bending and breaking. Bending a branch—or a child—takes time. You can break a branch in an instant. Parents with the right priorities know the difference. I can still see my grandmother grabbing a switch from the tree that stood in front of our home. I can see it so clearly, how she is stripping the leaves off slowly, methodically, unsmilingly, one by one. Once she got that far in the process I knew it was over. Once my grandmother started down the path of discipline, she never retreated.

Spare the rod, spoil the child. Most of the time she didn't even have to use the "rod." She just had to look at me with that special look. I'd look at her, and she'd look at me. Sometimes that is all it took. Other times she pulled the leaves from a switch one by one, even as my attitude of humility went into high gear. Then, with the skill of a Marine drill sergeant, grandmother would swing the switch in the air, causing it to emit a whistling sound. *Swish, swish, swish, swish.* She had my attention. Then it came. And as the switch found its target, she would say in rhythm what I had done wrong and what I needed to do about it.

My grandmother was the original rapper. In staccato she would say, "Tommmmy, didn't . . . I . . . tell. . . you" (that was four swings' worth) . . . "you . . . should . . . not . . . have . . . done . . . that" (six more). "Now . . . go . . . up . . . stairs . . . and stay . . . in . . . your . . . room . . .until . . . I . . . tell . . . you . . . to . . . present . . . yourself . . . down . . . stairs." For every word there was a swish. And with every question from grandmother, I would respond in a kind of antiphony, "Yes . . . you . . . did . . . Mama . . . I'm . . . real . . . sor . . .sorry. . . real . . . sor . . . ry." Why did she care so much? Because from day one she made me her number one. I was the most important person in her life.

The solution: make children a priority

Parents, if we are serious about making our children precious priorities, we'll have to decide *today* that we need Mom, not Montel. We need the child *connection*, not the *Love*

Connection. The tragedy is that *All My Children* got caught in a *Secret Storm* on the *Edge of Night* looking for the *Guiding Light* and ended up in *General Hospital.* So what is the lesson in this media madness for you and me? If your *Family Feud* leads you to *People's Court,* just remember that you asked for it. "Coke" used to be a soft drink. "Pot" was once something into which you placed a bouquet of flowers. "Gay" once meant "happy." A "closet" used to be something you went *into* and not something you came *out of.* "Crack" was the captivating sound of a bat hitting a baseball, not a substance that got you hooked overnight—or sooner.

**It will only get better when parents . . .
quit going along with the crowd and start
moving in the direction of the cross.**

My, how times have changed, but are we any better *for* the change? I don't think so. It will only get better when parents, who make their children a priority, quit going along with the crowd and start moving in the direction of the cross. We must give up to go up. There is *no express elevator to the top* when it comes to child raising—or to success in any field of personal endeavor. We all have to walk the stairs one step at a time. That means parents must start staying home, staying honest, and staying humble before the Lord.

- Parents with a child in mind must have principles that are constant.

- Parents with a child in mind must have priorities that never change.

- Parents with a child in mind must preach possibilities and promise.

- Parents with a child in mind must ponder the power of persistence.

- Parents with a child in mind must put the rod to work where necessary.

Fifteen things real parents do

Satan is not after our material; *he is after our minds.* He is not after our cars; *he is after our children.* He is not after our finances; *he is after our families.* He wants us to lie down and play dead—something thousands of parents are too willing to do. What's the solution? Where is the hope? Over the years, people have asked me to reiterate what I've shared often in my preaching and writing about the "Fifteen Things Real Parents Do." If repetition is the mother of learning, then perhaps this list is worth repeating:

1. Real parents discipline their children in a disciplined way. Real parents don't break up; they make up.

2. Real parents don't spoil the child and spare the rod.

3. Real parents know the best teaching is by example: where truth is caught, not taught.

4. Real parents are both tough-minded and tender-hearted.

5. Real parents recognize that a spanking in love is simply short-term pain for long-term gain.

6. Real parents take instead of send their children to church. Real parents do not prey on their children; they pray for them.

7. Real parents turn off the TV at suppertime because they realize if they don't turn off the news, their children may wind up in the news.

8. Real parents do not play around; they stay around.

9. Real parents do not rely on the lottery; they rely on the Lord.

10. Real parents do not divorce; they remain devoted.

11. Real parents love their children and know that God has a unique plan for their lives.

12. Real parents train them in the playpen so they won't end up in the state pen.

13. Real parents discipline them in the high chair so they won't end up in the electric chair.

14. Real parents know that if they take their children to the prayer chamber they will avoid the gas chamber.

15. Real parents provide their children with prayer and not pistols. They don't give them guns; they give them God.

One of the most beautiful expressions of how a child's sense of self-esteem is nurtured and developed is portrayed in the following prose piece by an unknown author. Mark these words well, my reader friend, and let their practical power be a constant challenge to you to remember that *by your personal example* your children learn whether or not they are a priority in your life—special angels sent to you from your Heavenly Father:

If a child . . .

If a child lives with criticism, he learns to condemn.

If a child lives with hostility, she learns to fight.

If a child lives with ridicule, he learns to be shy.

If a child lives with shame, she learns to feel guilty.

If a child lives with tolerance, he learns to be patient.

If a child lives with encouragement, she learns confidence.

If a child lives with praise, he learns to appreciate.

If a child lives with fairness, she learns justice.

If a child lives with security, he learns to have faith.

If a child lives with approval, she learns to like herself.

If a child lives with acceptance and friendship, he learns to find love in the world.

Children: priorities, not programs

Put yourself in the mind of your child for a moment. Now be that child, knowing that your parents regard you as their *number-one priority in life*. Nothing and no one is more important than you. Nothing and no one on earth will ever be more loved, cherished—and disciplined—than you. How does this make you feel? Do you feel special? I'm sure you do. Well, that's how I felt from the moment this Mama's Boy went to live with his grandmother in Cleveland. I was the most important person in her life and, in many ways, I was all she had.

Her daughter, my mother, had gone astray and had not fulfilled the dreams and hopes of my grandmother. My birth mother was a brilliant person who decided to be a rebel, go her own way, and live a self-centered life—a choice that eventually brought her to ruin. That was a great disappointment to her mother. Now, at an advanced age, the only person my grandmother had in her life was me, so she invested everything she had in me. I would like to believe that investment has not been in vain.

Now, with the advantage of having grown older and wiser, I see otherwise good people who are taking the exact opposite approach. I observe parents who seek to involve their boys and girls in any number of programs they feel will make their children a success. It is almost like watching the stock market. They keep hoping their children will produce. If they produce, the parents produce, and the parents are happy. But that does not necessarily make children a priority; it makes them a product.

Unfortunately, much of America's fascination with children excelling in sports is related to ego-driven parents, who live their less-than-eventful lives through the accomplishments of their children. I am suggesting a renewed, contrarian view: *to make our children a priority requires a major investment of self, not an inordinate outlay of money and expensive equipment.*

This renewed view of parenting demands time with a child in dialogue, communication, and prayer. My suspicion is that we would have a better present generation if parents spent as much time praying one-on-one with their children as they do overseeing them on soccer fields, baseball fields, and football fields. *Model choices and family values do not come from a glove and a bat; they come from teaching godliness,* which requires making prayer a priority, the Bible the book, and a family altar and family discussions places of refuge and retreat where the family learns to become a unit. Nothing can replace that. No sport, no program, no extracurricular activity will ever be as effective as the intimacy of the home.

**No sport, no program,
no extracurricular activity will ever be
as effective as the intimacy of the home.**

We must deal with our kids, not give them over to someone else to do the hard work of child raising. When we turn our children over to be raised by others—or when we give our boys and girls the remote control and say, "View what you want, little one," we abdicate our responsibility for raising that child. What kinds of values will your child learn in these situations? Are these influences contributing to how you *want your child to end up*? I believe we are over emphasizing the importance of extracurricular activities, events, and otherwise useful programs that are actually out of our control. That's why real parents don't rely on programs to raise their children; *they do the lion's share of the hard work themselves.* They give up their own priorities to make their children number one, and they monitor the outside programs they feel will best suit the emotional, physical, and spiritual growth of their children. In the process, they ask—and answer—the most important question of all: What better person to influence my child than the strongest man who ever lived, the Lord Jesus Christ?

Fathers, we, too, can be strong influences in the lives of our children. But to have that influence, we must do what real men do ...

Ten Things Real Men Do

from Boys To Men

1. Real men put away toys and pick up tools.

2. Real men do not just play—they pray.

3. Real men do not just party—they participate.

4. Real men do not just work out—they work!

5. Real men do not just date—they develop.

6. Real men who are single and saved know there is no such thing as safe sex—only saved sex. Any sex without the benefit and blessing of marriage is headed for physical and spiritual disaster.

7. Real men do not just love them and leave them—but they love them and help them, bless them and hold them, support them and take care of them.

8. Real men do not just father a baby—they become a father to a baby.

9. Real men take care of their babies—pay their support and pay it on time, in the right amount, with some extra thrown in.

10. Real men respect and cherish women as Daughters of the Nile, as descendents of Eve, an Afrikan woman who is the mother of all civilization. (This makes racism even more ridiculous, because black or white, we have the same mother!)

If there were any one person my grandmother talked about constantly and consistently, it was Jesus. She loved the Lord. She walked like a Christian, talked like a Christian, did business like a Christian, and she loved me like a Christian. No question about it: *she saw Jesus as the strongest man who ever lived.* He gave her the strength to stay morally pure; He helped her be a true friend to those in need. In my presence, she demonstrated by her life that she belonged to Jesus Christ, and that when her husband went to be with the Lord, the Lord became her husband. She devoted one hundred percent of her mind to her work, while giving one hundred percent of her life to Christian service. She modeled self-respect, decency, and propriety. For me, that was the reality with which I lived and was blessed.

If my grandmother were giving a mini seminar at a ladies' meeting and one of the women said, "Marilla, you're doing a good job with Tommy. How are you helping him become such a fine young man?" she would say, "Well, I just tell him that he has to live in such a way to please God, and if he pleases God, he'll please me. He knows the difference between right and wrong. And Tommy also knows that Jesus is the strongest man who ever lived. That's all he has to know." My grandmother also understood how Jesus told people that *the innocence of children, their lack of pretense, their honesty and humility is what they should be imitating—not the high-sounding nonsense of the Pharisees. She knew that a little child would always lead them.*

Now, these many years later, I honor my grandmother, who made me her priority; a little woman who stepped in for my mother, who no longer wanted me in her life; a woman who became my guiding light, my calming sight, and my warrior for all that was right. She could turn a collar and stretch a dollar. I never felt poor because she was rich in faith, love, and giving. She could cook, clean, sew, sing, iron, darn, garden, and run a business as well as anybody. No one could wipe away the tears and calm my fears like my grandmother. From a scratched knee to a broken heart to wounded pride, she was always at my side. She was my crossing guard and my body-guard. She'd never let those big, mean boys hurt her little Tommy. After all, I was Mama's boy.

Mama,

You are the queen of my heart. Your love is like tears from the stars. Mama, I just want you know that loving you is like food for my soul. You were there for me, to love and care for me when skies were gray. You were there to comfort me, and no one else could be what you have been to me. You were always there for me. For you, I was always a priority and never a program. Even when I was bad. You showed me right from wrong, and you took up for me when everyone was downing me. You always did understand, and you gave me the strength to go on. I know you are shining down from heaven, and I know we'll eventually be together—one sweet day.

With love and undying affection,

Mama's Boy

Chapter Nine

PRACTICING THE PRACTIAL POWER OF PRAYER

The church is looking for better methods.
God is looking for better men—
men of prayer that the Holy Ghost can use.
E. M. Bounds

Pray without ceasing.
1 Thessalonians 5:17

In an editorial written by grandmother titled "Forget," she talked about the importance of praying to remember all that is good and laying to rest all that is nonproductive, harmful, even sinful. It was always her prayer that she would allow past wounds inflicted upon her by the struggles of life to fade, and to recall only those events with which her Lord had blessed her. Yet, she freely admitted it would be a lifelong struggle for her prayers to be answered.

Because I was blessed to learn how to pray at my grandmother's knee, I caught her message early and often. It is now a theme I share with you as I lead this chapter with her editorial on the subject. In her own words, my grandmother expresses the importance of remembering the stars and paying less attention to the scars that life may have inflicted upon us:

Aren't there things in your life you never want to forget . . . then other things you'd give anything to forget? When a child, my Sunday school teacher had a big cardboard on the wall by our class with the word "forget," and she taught us always to forget the bad but remember the good.

For years I puzzled my childish brain to see if that were possible. I would remember how Mary saved my seat in the auditorium for devotional period . . . then I'd remember how Joe stuck his foot out in the aisle trying to trip me; then I'd think of Ethel bringing me apples on a stick that her mother made; and so on all week until Sunday, when I'd return saying: "I can't forget anything, I think of them all."

As I grew into womanhood, I began to see and understand life. I realized the principle our teacher was trying to instill in us. She was trying to dissolve the memory of evil, knowing it would grow into hate, and hate is deadly poison. But, I still cherish the kindness that others have done for me and trust they will never fade from my memory. . . . Then I think of wounds, too, that have hurt. I forgave . . . the wound has healed, but when I see the scar . . . I can't forget. I'll be honest, I find myself back in Sunday school still trying to solve that problem, "forget."

The practical power of personal prayer

As I read these words again, I find myself still saying, *Thank you, Mama, for what you taught me about kindness . . . about forgetting the bad and embracing the good . . . about the scars . . . about the wounds of life . . . about how to cope when I felt there was no hope . . . about a suffering Savior who was so terribly wounded, misunderstood, and afflicted for doing good . . . and about the importance of going to the Lord in prayer for all my needs.*

Now, as we begin to talk together about the practical power of praying for, with, over, and under our children, I would like to offer this personal prayer for you and for the children God has placed in your care:

Father, You have blessed us with these little angels, not for our abuse or our use, but as our inheritance, for they are the heritage of the Lord. In the depths of my heart, I feel for our children today. My heart cries out for them, because they are not only our future; they are our present. Father, in the name of Jesus, I pray and confess Your Word over our children. Father, You know what our children need, and You know what they're going through. You know how many things are being thrown at them, and how many challenges and forces are trying to destroy them. O God, the enemy is trying to steal and to destroy their lives, but in the name of Jesus we command the enemy to take his hands off every one of our little boys and girls and allow them to be free to become the children and adults You created them to be.

God, stir up in us a desire to be a part of their rescue and their nurture. And as I pray for the needs of our children, I also pray for their parents. Cause us to have the spirit of encouragement that embraces these mothers and fathers who are doing their best, under difficult circumstances, to give their children a home that honors You. Help these parents to teach their children, love their children, and, by their own lives, be an example of what it means to know Your Word. Help them to pray with, for, under, and over their little ones; help them to live lives of caring and compassion so that their children *catch* the greatest principles of life every day of their lives.

God, confirm in our minds that our children are our heritage. Help us remember that when we save a child, we save a church. When we save a church, we save a community. When we save a community, we save a nation, and when we save a nation, we save a world. Dear Jesus, bless our children. Bless them and protect them. We pray that the enemy will not rob them of their destiny, for our children are among the greatest human beings who will ever live on planet Earth. Thank You, Jesus, for blessing us with these little angels, and for giving us enough faith to teach them how to live and how to love.

We remember that You were once the Babe who confounded the elders of the temple at the tender age of twelve. You were the Messiah who picked up the little ones, and You tried to get Your point across that *children are important to You, for such is the Kingdom of God.* You persuaded people not to quench the spirits of children. You said *do not put them down, but give them to Me, for this is how the Kingdom operates.* For You, Jesus, children were and are a priority. Thank You for setting us straight. Thank You for how You love and cherish every little boy and every little girl. Thank You for the gift of children. Bless them and anoint them, in Your precious, Holy Name—in the blessed Name of the Babe of Bethlehem. Amen.

Fast forward to the twenty-first century, where Jesus is every bit as alive, as relevant, and as concerned about the well-being of our children as He was when he walked the dusty streets of Nazareth and ministered along the shores of Galilee. Jesus knew then, as He does now, that children *do* suffer from a lack of emotional contact with their parents. Children *do* suffer when no one prays for them and with them. Children who receive limited guidance from their parents *do* get into more difficulty—and have more trouble getting out of difficulty—than the child who is enveloped in a spirit of prayer. Jesus knew then, and He knows now, that when there is an epidemic of prayerlessness for our children, we all suffer.

**When we do not value prayer,
we cannot say we value God.**

So let's take the counsel of the Master to heart as we look at our own responsibility to pray. Because when we do not value prayer, we cannot say we value God. If you and I disapprove of the direction our culture is taking us today, could it be for our lack of prayer? If we do not like what our children do, the kids they hang with, the music they listen to, and how they dress, does not the lion's share of the responsibility fall upon us as parents? Do we dare to adopt the permissiveness of a cultural religion that has little time for God, and still have the temerity to hope for the best when it comes to our children's behavior?

My grandmother drummed into my head, from the day she picked me up at that railroad station in Cleveland to the day she died, that she would never stop praying for me, because that was the source of her power. *It is also the source of our power today.* It's just not good enough to holler up the stairs, "Johnny, did you say your prayers?" It's not good enough to ask, "Sally, do you want to go to Sunday school today?" There is no substitute for praying with, for, over, and under our children.

No prayer-by-osmosis

As an adult and a parent, I must confess that one of the gravest mistakes I ever made in raising three wonderful boys is that I failed to give them my best in this area of which I speak. For some reason, I felt since they were preacher's kids, that it would be *overkill* to pray with them and over them too much. After all, weren't they exposed to prayer every time the doors of the church opened? What a terrible mistake I made to think that. Perhaps you have raised your children with the same faulty thinking. You love God, you love the church, you love the fellowship of your brothers and sisters in Christ—and you feel that the prayers of the saints will somehow rub off on your children, that somehow the process of prayer-by-osmosis will touch their lives, change their hearts, and satisfy their spiritual needs. This is a huge mistake.

When we abdicate our responsibility to train our children by personal example, we will always pay the price. It is not the job of children to negotiate or some how "figure out" the extent of their spiritual training. It is *our* job as adults to train our children in the way they should go so that when they are old, they will not depart from the faith they have seen up close and personal in the lives of their parents.

People often ask me, "Dr. Benjamin, should I really help my child receive Jesus and become a Christian?" My answer is unequivocally, "Yes!" You can never be faulted for leading your children to the fresh water of God's grace, love, and mercy available in Jesus Christ. When we do not value prayer, we cannot say we value God. Why do I emphasize this? Because today our children are thirsty for meaning, and we dare not attempt to provide the Living Water they need *by remote control!*

You must go into their room and pray with them. You must put your arms around them, love them, and listen to their concerns so that you can pray powerfully and practically with them.

If you are going to pray for a child who is eight, nine, ten, eleven, twelve, or thirteen years old, you must go into their room and pray with them. You must put your arms around them, love them, and listen to their concerns so that you can pray powerfully and practically *with* them. That is the key: *with* them. Teach them how to pray by example. You can't do this from down in the basement, or while you're lying on the couch, remote control in hand, communicating with your children during the commercials—when you have nothing better to do. Nor can the Sunday school teacher do it. The preacher can't do it. The most well-meaning aunt and uncle can't do it—*unless you absolutely refuse to do it.* As a parent, you must pray with, for, over, and under your child. We are living in a society where we have discovered—as in the Columbine massacre—that parents are either afraid or hesitant about entering their children's personal space.

Since when do children have the right to make the rules? Sensitivity to privacy? Yes. But an abdication of responsibility for knowing what goes on behind closed doors—or in the confines of a sealed-off garage? Absolutely not. I may not be applauded for what I'm about to say, but I'll say it anyway: *No child in America has a private space in the home of his or her parents.* We need to invade those rooms, not with sinister suspicion, but with love, compassion, personal prayer, a personal touch, and personal suggestions about how that room can glorify God and not the devil.

Children want to trust their parents

In those quiet times of prayer and meditation with our children, we have the opportunity to remind them that we care about what they watch on television, what they read, who their friends are, what school they go to, how they dress, how they comb their hair, and how they relate to other adults. It is a golden opportunity to applaud them for attitudes that honor Jesus and others, for spirits that are strong and stable, and for hearts that are tender toward the hurting and the homeless. We have the privilege to inspire them more than they could ever dream, encourage them when they doubt their own abilities, and take great joy in seeing them succeed beyond their wildest imagination. This opportunity may not last long, but while it endures, *it is our most powerful position.* Not to respond positively to their deepest needs is to hand our children over to those who *will* listen to them, many of whom will not have our children's best interests at heart. The training of our children is not open to negotiation: it is the responsibility of parents, for without disciplined affection and prayerful understanding, parents forfeit a trust that may never be reclaimed.

I once read a story of a group of scientists and botanists who were exploring remote regions of the Alps in search of new species of flowers. One day they noticed through binoculars a flower of such rarity and beauty that its value to science was incalculable. The only problem was that the flower lay deep in a ravine with steep cliffs on both sides. To retrieve the flower someone had to be lowered over the cliff on a rope. A curious young boy was watching nearby, and the scientists told him they would pay him well if he would agree to be lowered over the cliff to retrieve the flower below. The boy took one long look down the steep, dizzy depths and said, "I'll be back in a minute." A short time later he returned, followed by a gray-haired man at his side. Approaching the botanist, the boy said, "Okay, I'm ready. I'll go over that cliff, but only if my daddy holds the rope." *Out of the mouths of babes, comes wisdom.*

**"I'll go over that cliff,
but only if my daddy holds the rope."**

Have you and I earned that level of trust from our children? Will your son or daughter freely hand you the rope when their challenges are greatest? Have your special times with your children been so life-changing that they will remember your prayers more than your preaching? Will they recall your times on the couch with an opened Bible more than the time you spent watching television? Perhaps you are raising a child whom you have never really valued. *It's not too late to confess your transgressions and open your heart to your boy or girl.* Maybe it's a child whom you have already raised, but because of your drive for material gain, you chose to put your most important gift on the back burner. Perhaps you found yourself rationalizing, *Look, it was only my way of making sure my child had everything, things I never had.* Again, this is a big mistake.

What does it matter if your child has all the toys in the store, but he or she doesn't have you? In the long view—and the long view is the only one that counts—your money, stock, real estate, and possessions will have zero value in comparison to the loss of relationship with your child. Perhaps you do not have children of your own, but you see children in your community who have no one who cares about them. They may be in a foster home, or perhaps they've been placed for adoption. Such children may never have experienced an adult praying with them and for them. Who knows? God may be leading you to take advantage of a new opportunity to bring a child to

Jesus simply because you cared enough to get involved.

Whatever you do—for your own child or for the child of another—you have the awesome privilege of making an eternal difference in the life of a boy or girl. If you have no desire to become personally involved, but you have resources that can help bring health, hope, and healing to a child, make a connection. Do something noble, in the name of Jesus. Here's what will happen in the process: *When you become so hungry for God's blessing on a child that it becomes your obsession, God will begin to do things for you He won't do for anyone else.* If you do not know precisely what to do to receive this blessing, you need only ask of your generous and benevolent Heavenly Father. He knows your heart, and He knows your deepest need. God insists that we ask His counsel, not because He needs information about our condition, but *because we need the spiritual discipline of relying on Him.*

**Whatever you do—
for your own child or for the child of another—
you have the awesome privilege of making
an eternal difference in the life of a boy or girl.**

Just as children rely on us for protection, so are we to rely on our Heavenly Father for His grace and mercy. You and I have our own assignments on this journey, which means there is no right or wrong way to pray—or to approach the One who loved us so much that He sent His Son to die in our place. But there is one serious command: *pray, and pray without ceasing.* What would our world be like if this is how we prayed for our children—without ceasing—while they are at home, at school, at play, at the movies, on the ball field, at their parties, at their concerts, while they're driving—*especially when they're learning to drive!*—and when they crawl under the covers at night, knowing that someone will soon come to their side, kneel down, and let the last words they hear at night be, *Jesus, bless our child. Know that this little boy means so much to me. Bless our little girl. Keep her pure. May she be an example for good in all she does. Now, dear Lord, give our child peace as she sleeps. May her dreams be filled with hope and goodness. Bless my little boy. Let him know that I love him more than life itself. Help our children know we will always be there for them whenever they need us. In the precious name of Jesus. Amen.*

A house bathed in prayer

Who would have known the day my grandmother picked me up at the Cleveland train station that I would be living with a prayer warrior who would intercede for me, with me, over, and under me every day for the rest of my life? Who could have guessed that at eight a.m. on that most important day of my life, a five-foot-tall African-American woman, a single parent whose husband had gone to be with the Lord, who had unsuccessfully raised a daughter, would take her little Tommy to the throne of grace day after day after day? My grandmother viewed prayer as an overlooked power. Untapped and unused, she saw too many parents sweeping it and its potential for good under the rug.

My grandmother was a prayer warrior, and she expected other parents to tap the same practical power of God's eternal presence. She saw, even in her generation, there were more players than pray-ers, more wimps than warriors, more arm-chair Christians than those who dared to meet the world head-on in the power of Jesus Christ. Years before our children had the sophisticated toys they have today, she saw parents giving children things that had virtually no value. Things were already beginning to become substitutes for relationships. *Such would not be the case with Mama's boy.*

My grandmother knew what life was all about, what raising a child was all about, and, for sure, she knew what prayer was all about. Whenever I asked my grandmother anything that demanded even a moment's reflection, she'd stop and say, "Tommy, let's pray about that. Now!" If you want to leave a legacy worthy of the name, pray with, for, under, and over your child. Do it now. Tomorrow. When they've left home, keep praying for your child. One of my most powerful memories is when I'd ask the question, "Mama, are you praying for me?" and she'd come back, "Huh? Did you say are you praying for me? Boy, why do you ask such a stupid question? Praying for you? Tommy, that's all I do is pray for you. And my prayers are bottled up in glory and will not go unanswered."

**"Tommy, that's all I do is pray for you.
And my prayers are bottled up in glory
and will not go unanswered."**

A prayer was always on her lips, and a prayer was always in her heart. I can still hear my grandmother say, "Tommy, let's pray about it before we do anything about it." Sometimes, when she couldn't get my attention, or she needed me to conform to her directive immediately, she would say, "Son, do we need to pray about that?" Sometimes I would say, "Sure do, Mama." At other times I would say, "Oh, Mama, we don't need to pray, let me just go ahead . . ." She would interrupt me and say, "No, we need to pray. Come on over here, Tommy." That's when she'd pull me over to her, grab my hands or grab my head or whatever she needed to do to get my attention, and say, "Lord, bless this child. Here he is again. I'm doing everything I can to help him, and still he's acting like I'm a stranger. Lord, I don't have time for this kind of foolishness. Lord, help this boy to help himself, because if he keeps doing what he's doing, he's going to get into deep trouble. Lord, show him the way, and let him know that You are with him, and that every victory is his if he will walk according to Your will. Lord, teach him the value of obedience, keep him safe today, and make him come home on time. In Jesus' name, I pray. Amen."

How could any grown man forget a prayer like that! She both inspired me and instructed me because she prayed with me and not just for me.

She both inspired me and instructed me because she prayed with me and not just for me.

I don't know how many nights this little woman would get down on her knees, weeping in prayer, as I would come in the door after the midnight hour—not so much weeping over me, but just bathing the house in fervent, effectual supplication to her Heavenly Father. Knowing her greatest strength came from within, she lived out the verse and the admonition of the apostle to *pray without ceasing*.

Even today I have difficulty praying by appointment. The church has its wonderful traditions—prayer jubilees, prayer revivals, and prayer meetings—and while these are important, sometimes I feel, as my grandmother did, that praying on schedule makes us stuffy and irrelevant, circumscribing the potency of prayer. It compartmentalizes our time with God. It makes folks think the only time they should pray is when the pastor or deacon or Sunday school teacher gives them permission to go to the throne of grace.

Recently, I was riding with Angel, an assigned driver, on my way to a meeting in Whittier, California. As we drove the overcrowded Los Angeles freeways, I observed that Angel was a man whose very countenance demonstrated submission and commitment to Jesus Christ. I could tell by his generous heart that he was a prayer warrior and grateful to God for the privilege of serving his Master and Lord. With traffic swirling around us, Angel drove us quietly and safely to our destination. Not speaking unless I spoke to him, he understood what it meant to be an "armor bearer." That was his joy, his ministry and his calling. Softly, trying not to be noticed, he was praying for me—only interrupted when we would fall into conversation. Then, when all was quiet, he would again lift his voice quietly to his Savior and Lord. Like my grandmother, Angel had tapped the power of praying without ceasing. Undoubtedly, many in America would probably think Angel was crazy—that he had a mental problem and could use some serious professional help. On the contrary, Angel is not the one who needs help. This caregiver had only positive thoughts for me, for those he cared about, and for the ministry to which he had been called. In the most loving way, Angel could only ask, "Bishop, how can I pray for you?"

"How can I help you?"

There was once a prominent, powerful businessperson in Indianapolis who had just gone through a tremendous reversal of fortune. Once high and mighty, he now found himself on the brink of financial disaster. When he called to invite me to lunch that day, I assumed he would be seeking my spiritual counsel regarding his deteriorating financial situation. Why else would he want to go to lunch with me—a pastor, not a financial consultant? We didn't know each other well, so we spent the first few minutes in casual conversation. Then, he broke through the small talk and asked, "Dr. Benjamin, how can I help you?" Since I'm a preacher, I'm seldom at a loss for words, but his question stunned me into silence. I was overwhelmed and hardly knew how to answer. I can't even remember what I said.

But wait . . . isn't this what we are all called to do? Aren't we supposed to help people and ask them if there's something going on that we can pray about? Isn't that what Christian service is all about? Isn't that what being a follower of Jesus is all about? And is this not what loving our children is all about?

Mama's Boy

Again, the question: what would our world be like if, every
day, we as adults sat down with our children and asked,
"Sweetheart, how can I help you today? How can I pray for
you as you get ready for school?" Do you think our world
would be a better place? What if parents responded to their
children as the man of God, in this poem, did in a most unlike-
ly setting?

> I sat amongst the people,
> a sheep within the herd,
> Waiting for the preacher
> to deliver up the Word.
> But first he called the children
> and prayed with them as one,
> And they scurried off to Sunday school
> the moment he was done.
>
> And then we saw a picture
> I know I'll not forget
> As the preacher's little daughter
> threw her arms around his neck.
> She kissed him many, many times,
> adoringly she clung.
> I realized in that moment
> that the message had begun.
>
> God didn't need our schedule,
> an agenda, or a list.
> He showed us each a million things
> within a child's kiss.
> The preacher wasn't hurried.
> His demeanor wasn't rushed.
> He loved his little child
> and the congregation hushed.
>
> His tender little daughter
> had forgotten we were there.

Adoration for her father
was her one and only care.
It was just a fleeting moment
but it hung there just the same.
She looked so very tiny
hanging on this grown man's frame.

No sermon could have said it,
no song could capture this.
I learned about my Father's love
in a little child's kiss.
God wants me to come running.
He wants to pull me in.
The love He gives outweighs the thoughts
of work and time and sin.

I so adore my Father.
We're not meant to be apart.
He shines His light all over
my transparent, needy heart.
No matter that I'm feeble.
No matter what they say.
I feel the warmth of all His love
when I bow my head to pray.

I'm just a little child.
My Father's love is huge.
He saves me each and every day
and offers me refuge.
He loves me in my weakness.
He loves me in my strife.
I cling to Him for comfort
and I cling to Him for life.

When the going gets tough, and the challenging road of child rearing gets rough, I urge you to recall the comforting words of Hebrews 12:1: "Therefore, since we are surrounded by such a great cloud of witnesses, let us throw off everything that hinders and the sin that so easily entangles, and let us run with perseverance the race marked out for us" (NIV).

When you seem to have lost your focus and have encouraged "things" that have little or no eternal worth to take precedence over what has true value, remember the words of Hebrews 12:2, which demands that we "fix our eyes on Jesus, the author and perfecter of our faith, who for the joy set before Him endured the cross, scorning its shame, and sat down at the right hand of the throne of God" (NIV).

When you've forgotten your first love, allowed your heart for Christ to grow cold, and find your daily actions bring dishonor to your Heavenly Father, let the words of 1 Peter 1:13-15 be your constant prayer: "Therefore, prepare your minds for action; be self-controlled; set your hope fully on the grace to be given you when Jesus Christ is revealed. As obedient children, do not conform to the evil desires you had when you lived in ignorance. But just as he who called you is holy, so be holy in all you do" (NIV).

We add enormous value to everything we praise. Praise your children, pray for them, pray with them, pray over them and under them. Add value to their lives by making them feel they're the most important people on the face of the earth. They are!

The Creator gave you dominion over the earth. *Live and love as if this were true in your life and in your relationships.*

We add enormous value to everything we praise. Praise your children, pray for them, pray with them, pray over them and under them. Add value to their lives by making them feel they're the most important people on the face of the earth. They are!

Give your best at all times—and be a cheerful giver. You will be absolutely amazed how God will return his blessing to you manyfold.

And whatever you do, do it with a grateful heart. Grandma wrote, "If we thanked Providence more and appreciated our blessings more, the happier we would be . . . all of which would give us a little heaven of our own. Life can be beautiful if we would just let it be." This powerful praying black woman knew that happiness always comes from within, and that it is our spiritual privilege to tap the practical power of prayer to use that inner joy to change our world—one person, one child—at a time.

Ten years ago I preached a sermon called "My Name is Jabez." I preached it in the first person and took on the character and consciousness of Jabez in 1 Chron. 4:9-10. Long before Bruce Wilkinson's wonderful little book on the subject I began praying: "Lord, bless me indeed. Enlarge my territory. Keep your hand on me. And keep me from all evil.

And like Jabez, God has answered my prayers!

You see, I know what prayer can do. I am a living testimony. After all, I am Mama's boy.

Chapter Ten

AIM HIGH . . . FINISH STRONG

*Two caterpillars were crawling across the grass when
a butterfly flew over them. They looked up, and
one nudged the other and said, "You couldn't get me
up in one of those things for a million dollars."*

> *I can do all things through Christ,
> who strengtheneth me.*
> Philippians 4:13 (KJV)

The late Dr. Benjamin Elijah Mays, revered minister and educator at Morehouse College, penned these immortal words: "It must be borne in mind that the tragedy of life doesn't lie in not reaching your goal. The tragedy lies in having no goal to reach. It isn't a calamity to die with dreams unfulfilled, but the calamity is not to dream. It is not a disgrace not to reach the stars, but it is a disgrace to have no stars to reach for. Not failure, but low aim is sin."

William Augustus Jones tells the story of a man who sailed solo from the New York harbor around the world in fourteen months only to get within one hundred yards of the Statue of Liberty and drown. This is the commentary on too many lives today. We may aim high but we don't finish strong; sometimes we do not finish at all. My grandmother always encouraged me to aim high *and* finish strong. She used to say, "Reach for the moon and you will never grab dirt." As usual, she was right.

Martin Luther King Jr. said it best: "If it falls your lot to be a street sweeper, you should sweep streets like Michelangelo painted pictures, or Beethoven composed music, or Shakespeare wrote poetry." Aim high and finish strong. Sweep streets so well that all the host of heaven and earth will say, "Here lived a street sweeper who swept his job well."

Good-bye to fear and failure

My grandmother would remind me that if I was always afraid the worst would happen, then my own thoughts would help to bring it about. By her life she showed me that *fear is the wrong use of imagination*. It is anticipating the worst, when God wants to provide His best. And my grandmother was right. She was also on target when she told me that our God is stronger than handcuffs. Stronger than iron gates. Stronger than armed guards. Stronger than any weapons Satan can throw at God's children. She would remind me that God lives in both a prison and a palace, and that He unlocks the vaults of heaven and opens His abundant storehouse, which *includes everything that you need, Tommy!*

Fear is the wrong use of imagination.

In her mini messages to me, she'd say things like, "Son, never put yourself in a position where you think that you can't. Never say never. Stay on your knees. Don't get locked up in the prison of yourself, because you don't have to be in a real jail to be behind bars." Again, Mama was right. She knew that bondage comes in at least fifty-seven varieties. We marry to be happy and create a home environment that brings glory to God—but then we fail to finish strong. We have children whom we dedicate to the Lord. We start out loving them, praying with, for, over, and under them, and then, for some reason, we back off—and we fail to finish strong. We pursue our individual careers to make money, become people of influence, with the goals of being a provider and protector for our family—but material gain and the seduction of the world and its distractions get in our way, and we fail to finish strong. What's the problem? Why do we start out with such great God-given potential, and so often fail to remain the people God created us to be?

I can still hear Mama say something like, "God does not cause your pain, but He allows it to come to make you strong. God does not cause problems, but He allows troubles to cross your path to get your attention and get you to depend on nobody but Him. He's tired of you depending on everybody but Him. But sometimes He has to let you get in a corner so you can see that there's nobody who will help you but God. Some people are so numb that God has to turn up the fire for them to really see Him."

Shaped by my past; preaching from my passion

The rich faith in God that I picked up from my grandmother—much like the joyous living young Timothy saw in the life of his grandmother Lois—has given me a much-needed perspective in understanding my own pain and adversity. I suspect that if I had not been cut loose at age five, felt the rejection of my parents, and gone through what I went through, I would undoubtedly hold a different perspective on children and their troubles, on children and their abandonment, on children and their loneliness, on children and the abuse they suffer at the hands of those who are supposed to love and nurture them.

No question about it: I'm preaching out of my passion, produced by my pain. I was wounded early in life, wounded deeply. Now I'm called to bandage up the wounds of my parishioners and others. Sometimes I'm reminded that, because of their pain, I, too, have pain, but that must not prevent me from giving them my best, which includes my experience and how I have acknowledged adversity not as a problem, but as a possibility. God puts us in painful situations to develop us as persons. For me, pain has been at the center of my transition from being a boy to becoming a man.

I hurt for boys whose maturity gets mugged by materialism.

I hurt for boys who are raped by racism.

I hurt for boys who allow themselves to become gutted by greed.

I hurt for boys who contract AIDS before they come of age.

I hurt for boys who get into crack before they get into the church.

I hurt for boys who get into gangs before they get into God.

I hurt for boys who get into hip-hop before they get into holiness.

I hurt for boys who get into pistols before they get into prayer.

I hurt for boys who get into jail before they get into Jesus.

**What I've been through is not
nearly as important as what I'm going to.**

My hurt has pushed me to help. It has made me a better man because I can now reflect on what I've been through and I can share with others. The good news is that *what I've been through is not nearly as important as what I'm going to.* I've been wounded to heal. I would have no real healing anointing unless I had been hurt. I am a wounded healer. My rejection has been used by God to make me a more effective healer. I don't believe anything that happens in this universe happens by accident. I'm so glad the Bible says that *all things work together for good to them who love the Lord and who are called according to His purpose.*

All things work together for good

Paul says in Romans 8:28 that there's nothing in this world that can happen to you as a believer in Christ that God does not know about and does not use ultimately for your good. So if you can wait on the Lord and be of good courage, He will strengthen your heart by showing you that what men intended for evil, He intended for good, and that no weapon formed against you shall prosper. We are talking about how God works, and how His ways are not our ways, nor are His thoughts our thoughts. God works mysteriously, but it is always for our good. Neither you nor I can ever fully explain suffering, except to say that, ultimately, God intends it for good.

Sometimes it's difficult for me to keep that perspective in mind. Because I often ask myself, *Why am I doing this? Why do I spend hours interviewing children who have become first-time offenders? Why do I so much want them to have a second chance?* It's because somebody gave me a second chance and it's because these children are not bad. Human evil is a developmental process, and we all become evil slowly over time through a long series of poor choices. These children have made poor choices, and I choose to come alongside them and be an influence for good. I want to try to show them that life is not a dead-end street, for I, too, was once lost, but now I'm found. I, too, was once blind, but now I see. For me it was nothing short of amazing grace when a little five-foot-tall woman caught my falling soul, looked beyond my faults, and saw my needs.

My passion is the foundation that supports everything I write about, teach, and preach. I've learned that whatever makes me cry is something I need to address, because I know I'm not alone in my pain. I used to think it was a cliché, but now I know that a person really does have to walk a mile in someone else's moccasins to be able to identify. For that reason, I can now see how my miles of unseen misery have helped pour more compassion on people who are hurting— especially our children. Like Smokey Robinson, "I follow the tracks of my own tears." Whatever makes you cry is something you have been assigned to heal.

Pain will be with us as long as God gives us breath, but that's no reason to quit.

That's why my life's message is that *it's always too soon to quit*. Pain will be with us as long as God gives us breath, but that's no reason to quit. Failure, defeat, and discouragement will dog our steps until the day Jesus returns to take us home—but that's no reason to quit. When we finally understand that where there's a problem there's a solution—as my grandmother drilled into this young man's head—we'll never find an excuse to quit. William Gladstone, the renowned prime minister of England, said, "No man ever became great or good except through many and great mistakes." Abraham Lincoln failed in almost everything he tried to do. Even his marriage was unsuccessful. Poor, and with only six months of formal schooling, he had no well-heeled friends to turn to for financial assistance; his closet had no fancy clothes; some of his "friends" told him he was downright ugly. Yet, he met his challenges head-on, and we all know the rest of the story of Honest Abe. God never meant for our lives to be a resting place. Instead, He designed them to be a testing place. The bigger message for you and me is that failure—any failure—can be a blessing if we accept it in the proper light.

Yes, I still cry—often in silence—but I do cry. No longer for my own pain, but for the pain of others. I cry when I see a child abused. I cry when people don't listen to their children. I cry when otherwise well-meaning parents send their children to church instead of bringing their little ones to God's house. I cry when I see mothers and fathers fail to finish strong. I cry when I see a television program that promotes promiscuity. I cry when the self-esteem of a child is crushed under the weight of a parent whose life is consumed with alcohol and drugs. I cry when I hear the lyrics of songs that promote rape, murder, incest, and hatred. And my suspicion is that you, my reader friend, cry too.

Feeling alone among a cast of thousands

I would now like to be candid about something I've never spoken of before. Sometimes I still feel very much alone. Yes, I'm a pastor of a large church; yes, I've spoken before tens of thousands of people; yes, I have a wonderful family. Yet, I often still feel alone. When my grandmother died, I had the strangest feeling that the blanket that kept me warm for so long had been lifted and that I was now uncovered. Even though I had a congregation of thousands and had made acquaintances from around the world, I still felt like I was on my own. Within three years, I lost three very important people in my life: in 1989, my mother died; in 1990, my father died; and in 1991, my grandmother went to be with Jesus. I was suddenly left without anyone. Even though I was now an adult, I was not prepared to be left alone. Sounds like that train ride all over again.

I remember asking God, "Why is it that I have nobody? No family. No brothers. No sisters. No cousins. No nieces. No nephews." God probably shook His head as He said, "Tommy, you have a wife and three wonderful children; now, isn't that enough? Aren't you blessed?" With that admonition from above, I repented. As I later reflected on my mountain of blessings—and ruminated on what I had, not what I had lost—my hand went to my pen, and I wrote these words to the three boys God sent to live with Beverly and me . . .

A love note to my grown children

My Dear Sons,

As I write you, my heart is happy because I have been blessed with three wonderful sons. My heart is heavy because I know I didn't do enough, say enough, be enough to prepare you for the future. I hope one day I will stand tall enough in your memory to merit the words of Edgar Guest, who said, "I know he was as fine a dad as any boy ever had. What I didn't know until too late was the depth of his wisdom and the magnitude of his sacrifice."

First and foremost, Daddy loves his boys, and if you remember one thing from this letter, remember I love you more than you know and probably more than I show.

You were born to make the world a better place to live. Your true identity is a child of God, and yet each of you is special. Jesus said, "Without Me you can do nothing" (John 15:5, NKJV). Howard Thurman, one of my mentors, said to me, "When you and God become one, all of life's resources begin to flow toward you." Discover your purpose and you discover your power.

I have found that if you do what you love to do, then you will do it well and everything else will follow. What you really want to do is help people and be happy. Jesus said, "Seek first the kingdom of God and His righteousness, and all these things shall be added to you" (Matthew 6:33, NKJV).

The most important choice you will ever make is to choose **Jesus Christ.** God chose you, but you must choose God as your eternal Father and your King. You must submit to your King, Jesus, in everything. As I have told you, your quality of life depends on the choices you make. Your great-grandmother used to say, "If you make your bed of rocks, you will have to lie on them." I said in my book *Boys To Men,* which I dedicated to you, "There are no bad boys, just bad choices." I also said, "Success comes in cans: I can, I can, I can."

The second choice is your **lifelong mate.** Your wife will be the mother of your children and your divinely designated helper in your family and every other area. My advice is similar to Gen. Colin Powell's advice to the West Point cadets: "Marry high!" I agree, except I would be more specific: marry a woman who loves God more than she loves you. That's exactly what I did when I married your mother.

The third choice is your **friends.** Choose them carefully because the people you draw to you and around you are the soil in which you grow. Make sure your friends love and serve God, and if they don't, introduce them to Jesus. Be courageous enough to make new friends if the old ones don't cause you to grow and glow. Someone has said, "Don't spend major time on minor people." Please don't.

The fourth choice is your **attitude.** Chuck Swindoll says, "Attitude is everything." Carter G. Woodson, the father of African-American history, declared, "If you can control a man's thinking, then you can control his action." The proverbial writer observed, "As he thinks in his heart, so is he" (Proverbs 23:7, NKJV). That's why it is important to get all the education you can. You should read, travel, and explore. Expand your mind!

The fifth choice is **giving.** Giving is the secret to abundantly receiving. Motivator Zig Ziglar says, "Give enough people in this life what they need, and they will give you all you need." Jesus was even more succinct when He said, "The measure you give will be the measure you get" (Matthew 7:2, NRSV). Adopt giving as a lifestyle. You are blessed to be a blessing.

I know it wasn't easy to be a PK (preacher's kid), but never discount the truth I preached to you and others. And never think because you were raised in the church you don't need the church. Soon I will be in heaven, and my prayer is that you don't forget to live your life and express your faith in such a way that we will spend eternity together.

You have given me so much joy and so much fulfillment as a dad. At the age of five, I was put on a train leaving St. Louis, Missouri, to live with my grandmother in Cleveland, Ohio, because my parents were getting a divorce. I felt rejected and unprotected. I promised the Lord I would do better with my sons. I have been the husband of one wife, your mother, for more than thirty years. We have loved each other through thick and thin with a lifelong commitment. Keeping your word is very important. It's called integrity.

Keep God first in your life. Love God with everything you have. Love your neighbor as you love yourself. Remember you are special, and you can make a difference in your lifetime. Keep a positive attitude. Give: it's the key to life. Serve: it's the key to peace. Pray: it's the key to power. Love: it's the key to God. Take care of your parents when they are unable to care for themselves.

Aim high in all you do, because Benjamin E. Mays, the educator, has said it well: "Low aim is sin!" You used to chuckle when I would say this, but it's still true:

"Bite off more than you can chew and chew it.

Do more than you can do and do it.

Hitch your wagon to a star.

Take a seat and there you are!"

Daddy loves his boys, and all I ever wanted was the best for you. Aim high!

Love,

Dad[8]

The past is a prologue to something greater

Were it not for my grandmother, I could not have written this love note to my three precious sons. That's because she taught me that making children a priority automatically makes one a protector; bathing children in prayer automatically gives

---

[3] "Choices," contained in *From a Father's Heart*, Dan Reiland (Nashville: Thomas Nelson Publishers, 1999), pp. 69–72.

them to God; and practicing good parenting skills insures a measure of success. Unfortunately, parenting skills are more caught than taught, so when there is no teacher, it becomes hard to pass great wisdom on to your child. That's why the vicious cycle of "kids having kids" and younger parents raising children by themselves continues to be one of the greatest challenges our society faces today. What would Mama say about how to respond to our dilemma? I think she would say that *the more you give, the more God gives to you.* What you are seeing is just part of the promise. When you give your life to others—especially to children—you won't be able to count the blessings. They'll overtake you. For sure, Mama would say, "To God be the glory!"

The more you give, the more God gives to you.

To this point, I believe my life has simply been God's preparation for what is yet to come. And those who know tell me that it's just going to get better. And that goes for you too. You and I are still on our journey with Christ. There's still work to do. We're not home yet. But when we do get to heaven, we're going to sing and shout. "Can't nobody in heaven put us out." No more rejection. Only acceptance. People can close the door on us down here. They can reject us, neglect us, and object to everything we try to do. But when we get to heaven, all that will change. Meanwhile, it's always too soon to quit, and with the help and mercy of our loving Heavenly Father, we will continue to aim high so we can finish strong. That's the goal of this Mama's boy.

Yes, I am a Mama's boy, but not the kind who is so sheltered by his caregiver that he's been defined by her. There are some who are mama's boys in the sense they are either effeminate or soft or hiding behind a woman's skirts. Praise God, I've become a Mama's boy who became a developed man, a strong man, a man my grandmother insisted would become a *whole* man. This Mama's boy owes everything to the Lord Jesus Christ and his grandmother. I'm saying to you that when it's all said and done, I'm proud to be called Mama's boy. I belong to Jesus, but I am a product of my Mama, who insisted I aim high so I could finish strong. How could I help becoming who I've become when all I'd hear was Mama's voice saying, "Jesus in the morning, Jesus in the evening, Jesus all night long"?

A letter from Mama

Not only did my grandmother love me as her son, but she also cared passionately about her many friends—one of whom was a woman she loved as a daughter, Betty Howard, an Indianapolis educator. Recently, Betty was gracious enough to share a stack of personal letters with me, all written in my grandmother's own hand. As I read them, my heart kept going back to that early morning on a railroad platform, when grandma welcomed a confused little boy to the big city of Cleveland. Why did my mind go back to that special day? Because what my grandmother was that day at the train station *is the person she remained to her dying day.* With Mrs. Howard's permission, I would like to share a portion of one of her letters to her "daughter" Betty. I think you will quickly fathom the heart of the woman who called me her Mama's boy.

My Dear Child,

Just know you are special to me. Was I happy to hear your voice! Oh, I'm so glad He watches over us all. As my dear old grandmother used to say, "My God is writing all the time. He sees all you do and hears all you say, for my God is writing all the time."

Oh, I thank Him for His goodness to me. I praise Him for just being so mindful of me. To me, it seems surprising how people on the street, anywhere I go, seem so thoughtful of me. I just seem surrounded by love. Yes, and I know it's

His precious hand. Don't think I don't thank and praise Him for it, as it could be so different. I know I am in His care. Storms arise, but He is master of all storms. He asks us in His Word, 'Is my arm any shorter?' I just answer Him, 'No, Lord.' So many things have turned out differently than what I expected in life, but here I go again—*All things will work for good for me because I know I love the Lord.*

He can't and He won't lie. He is God. . . . Keep your chin up and looking to Him, for the way this whole world is rocking, I believe it won't be long before He will return.

With heaps of love,

Mother Jackson

People get ready, there's a train a comin'

What's that sound I hear? Sounds like a train coming down the tracks. Yes, it is a train—the clickety-clack of the Kingdom train. *Is that you, Mama? Is it you there in the distance?* I can't see you clearly yet, but I know you're there. I love you, Mama, and I'll be seeing you soon. I don't know when I'll get there, but I know you'll be standing by, waiting for me as that celestial coach pulls into heaven's station. *What's that, Mama? Will I recognize you?* Of course I'll recognize you, Mama. I don't know much about the height of people in heaven, but I'll be looking for my Mama, who stands about five feet high and whose smile can light up the skies.

Don't worry, Mama, I'll know you the minute my feet strike Zion. But this time, I know you won't be greeting me wearing your old, worn, tattered coat—like the one you had on when you received me that blessed day in Cleveland so long ago. This time, I figure you'll be dressed up nice and pretty in a long white robe, all radiant and bright. And when I hear the porter say, "Heaven . . . Heaven," I'll look for you from the window, and step down the steps—on my own, this time—on to those great golden streets you used to always sing about. I know I'll see you there, looking for your Tommy. Then, after we've had our long, heavenly hug, I've got a feeling you'll step back a bit, look me up and down real good, like you always did, and you'll probably say once again, through tears, *"How's Mama's boy?"*

This time I can answer with confidence: "Mama, I am doing fine. The road has not been easy and you never said it would be, but I am here! Thank God I made it by His Grace and your love. I could not pay you back for your love, but I did try to pass it on. I made it."

After all, I am Mama's boy.

To order additional copies of *Mama's Boy*

or other books by Tom Garrott Benjamin, Jr.

Visit www.tombenjamin.com
mamasboy@tombenjamin.com

Vision International Publishing, Inc.
P.O. Box 18088
Indianapolis, IN 46218-0088

1-800-VIP-9695
(1-800-847-9695)

Other books available by Tom Garrott Benjamin, Jr.:

Boys To Men

The Home Alone Syndrome

To Order Additional Copies of

Mama's Boy

by

Tom Garrott Benjamin, Jr.

(for a Ministry Gift of at least $14.95 per book)

Check with your local bookstore or order on this form.

Name _____

Street _____

City/State/Zip _____

Telephone _____

E-mail address _____

Title	Quantity	Ministry Gift per book	Total
Mama's Boy		$14.95	$
		Subtotal	$
		Postage/Handling per book	$ 5.00
		Total	$

Return order form along with check or money order payable to:

Vision International Publishing, Inc.
P. O. Box 18088
Indianapolis, IN 46218-0088

Telephone Orders may be placed to 1-800-847-9695
(Quantity discounts available)

❑   Mastercard

❑   Visa

Account # _____

Expiration Date: Month _____ Year _____

Signature _____

Great for Men's or Women's Ministry Group studies!

PLEASE ALLOW 2 WEEKS FOR DELIVERY